WRESTLING WITH THE DEVIL

■ ■ ■

WRESTLING
WITH THE DEVIL
LEX LUGER

WITH JOHN D. HOLLIS

THE TRUE STORY OF A WORLD CHAMPION PROFESSIONAL WRESTLER—
HIS REIGN, RUIN, AND REDEMPTION

TYNDALE
MOMENTUM

AN IMPRINT OF TYNDALE HOUSE PUBLISHERS, INC.

Visit Tyndale online at www.tyndale.com.

Visit Tyndale Momentum online at www.tyndalemomentum.com.

TYNDALE is a registered trademark of Tyndale House Publishers, Inc. *Tyndale Momentum* and the Tyndale Momentum logo are trademarks of Tyndale House Publishers, Inc. Tyndale Momentum is an imprint of Tyndale House Publishers, Inc.

Wrestling with the Devil: The True Story of a World Champion Professional Wrestler—His Reign, Ruin, and Redemption

Edited by Bonne Steffen

Cover designed by Erik M. Peterson

Interior designed by Dean H. Renninger

This work is a memoir. Some dialogue has been recreated.

Published in association with the literary agency of Legacy, LLC, 501 N. Orlando Avenue, Suite #313-348, Winter Park, FL 32789.

Library of Congress Cataloging-in-Publication Data
Luger, Lex.
  Wrestling with the devil : the true story of a world champion professional wrestler—his reign, ruin, and redemption / by Lex Luger with John D. Hollis.
     pages cm
  Includes bibliographical references.
  ISBN 978-1-4143-7872-5 (hc)
  1. Luger, Lex. 2. Wrestlers—United States—Biography. I. Hollis, John D. II. Title.
  GV1196.L84A3 2013
  796.812092—dc23
  [B]   2013009930

Printed in the United States of America

19   18   17   16   15   14   13
7   6   5   4   3   2   1

I DEDICATE THIS TO YOU, THE READER, THAT MY STORY MAY INSPIRE YOU TO **BUILD YOUR LIFE UPON THE ROCK.**

■■■

JESUS SAID, "ANYONE WHO LISTENS TO MY TEACHING AND FOLLOWS IT IS WISE, LIKE A PERSON WHO BUILDS A HOUSE ON SOLID ROCK" (MATTHEW 7:24).

CONTENTS

FOREWORD

When I first met Lex Luger, I didn't like him at all. The guy may have been "The Total Package"—famous for having the greatest physique of anyone in pro wrestling—but I thought he was a rude and arrogant jerk. While I was still an unknown in the sport at the time, Lex was already a headliner and earning big bucks. I'd often see him at the gym when I arrived for my early-morning workout, but we didn't say much to each other at first. Neither of us was there to make friends. All we cared about was getting to be number one in the ring—no matter what it took.

But over the years, I got to know Lex well as we wrestled as both partners and foes. His bodybuilder's physique wasn't merely for show; he had genuine freakish strength. We developed a strong mutual respect and a close personal friendship. In our extremely competitive and risk-filled industry, you needed someone you could count on to watch your back. Lex became that person for me, and I for him.

I remember rushing to the hospital after Lex was in a motorcycle accident that could have killed him. Even though I was there to reassure him that everything was going to be okay, I was deeply concerned. His arm was so mangled that I couldn't imagine any doctor being able to put it back together. But in the end, it was okay. We were there for each other, like brothers. I figured that was the way it was always going to be.

But things got rocky. Lex and I, like many pro wrestlers, were living secret lives on the road that we never wanted our families to know about. We were facing (and falling into) every temptation imaginable. Drugs, alcohol, women, you name it. The world grew so dark that everything else fell apart—including our friendship.

In 1998, after finally losing the biggest wrestling match of my life against God, I gave my life to Jesus Christ. He began transforming me from the inside out. When I tried to reconnect with Lex then, he wasn't interested. But I never stopped trying to reach out. The only time he called me was when Elizabeth Hulette died from an overdose of alcohol and pills—a tragic event that rocked not just the wrestling community but Lex's own world.

Lex Luger—one of the toughest and most powerful pro wrestlers—was wrecked and shattered. To the world, it seemed like his story was over. But God was just getting started with Lex.

This book is about how Lex Luger got from where he was then— a convicted felon, a womanizer, a drug user, a worshiper of self and money and fame—to a man who experienced one of the most dramatic and miraculous transformations I've ever seen. *Wrestling with the Devil* is a wild ride, a behind-the-scenes look at Lex's glory days of wrestling, the tragic crash that followed, and his remarkable journey of discovering true strength.

Today, the once-Herculean body is battered and frail. He may have lost his physical power, but spiritually he's a giant for God. He's a perfect example of what the Bible refers to as a "new creation." As it says in 2 Corinthians 5:17 (NKJV), "If anyone is in Christ, he is a new creation; old things have passed away; behold, all things have become new."

I have never known anybody stronger than Lex Luger—in or outside the ring. He has truly wrestled with the devil. This book is his story of victory.

STEVE BORDEN, AKA STING
MARCH 2013

PROLOGUE

The pain was excruciating and sudden, jolting me awake in the early morning hours.

It felt like someone was gashing me with a butcher knife or searing me with a branding iron. *What's happening? How did someone get in my room? Is this for real, or am I dreaming?*

I was no stranger to pain. I had sustained plenty of nasty injuries throughout my life. Some were particularly unique to wrestling. Like the time the Big Show snatched me with his massive hands, lifted me ten feet in the air, and choke-slammed me through a table onto the concrete floor. Or the many times I was battered and bloodied with a steel chair.

But this was different, an intense agony unlike anything I'd ever experienced. I had learned to push through pain, but this . . . I had to squeeze my eyes shut to hold back the tears.

Maybe if I just change position, the sharpness will be less acute or the burning will subside. Did I lie down wrong? I'd had twinges over the previous weeks, but the pain that was now shooting down my neck between my shoulder blades was a hundred times worse. So I tried to adjust.

And then the unthinkable reality hit me: I couldn't move.

It felt as if there were giant suction cups on my back, pulling me down, down, through the sheets, through the mattress, through the bed frame. My body was heavier than a dead weight, like someone had played a malicious prank while I was sleeping and encased me in cast iron.

What the—? I gritted my teeth and winced. I needed to try shifting positions again. *Yes.* I could move my head and shoulders somewhat, but nothing else. If I could just roll off the side of the bed and get on my knees, I figured I might be able to reach the phone. Then I could call for help. I didn't know what else to do.

I began to rock cautiously, slowly inching my way to the edge of the queen-size bed, thankful for even this extremely limited movement. *I can catch myself with my left arm and break my fall.*

My plan worked, kinda. But I forgot my left arm was useless.

I plummeted to the floor like a rock, landing on my back between the two beds in my room with my head pinned against the nightstand. The imaginary, powerful suction cups were intact, now pulling me down, down, through the carpet, through the floor.

When I tried to get up, nothing happened. I couldn't pivot my head or move a muscle, other than blinking my eyes and opening my mouth. The irony of the situation didn't escape me: My life had been based on physical prowess, but now I couldn't even lift a finger.

I was terrified; I had never felt so helpless.

Crumpled against the nightstand, with my head twisted at an awkward angle and my chin pressed into my chest, I could barely breathe. *I'm in serious trouble. Is this how I'm going to die, alone on a hotel room floor?* My breaths grew more shallow.

"Help! Please, help me!" I pushed out the cry with all my might, but it merely brushed my lips in a faint whisper. Even if someone had been lying right next to me, my words would have been barely audible.

The telephone sitting twenty inches above me on the nightstand seemed miles away. *Is this really how it's going to end? That will make a great headline: "'The Total Package' Returned to Sender."*

Why is this happening? What is going on? I implored the darkness. I waited for an answer, my mind starting to drift, rewinding and fast-forwarding through my life, piecing it together. There had to be clues.

1
BUFFALO BOY

"You'll never catch me!"

From the time I was a small boy growing up in Buffalo, New York, I loved to run. I'd race up and down the sidewalk as fast as I could for hours. It probably looked strange to passersby, but the way the wind felt on my face when I accelerated gave me a deep sense of joy. Maybe, in reality, I was releasing pent-up energy. But whatever the reason, I didn't stop. Mom would say that I was like "greased lightning." It definitely was an asset in neighborhood games of tag—no one could get their hands on me. If anyone got close, I'd swerve at the last second and watch my pursuer stumble and fall. I prided myself on never being tagged "it"—unless I wanted to be. And if I did, I would run circles around everyone else. When I was old enough for a bike, I'd speed around the block, pedaling so hard I should have been airborne.

In the 1950s, Buffalo was still a blue-collar steel town, known for its proximity to Niagara Falls and what would become its world-famous Buffalo wings. But my family was defined by something different: music.

Roger Pfohl and Marion Monteith were both students at the University of Buffalo when they met. My dad was a brilliant musician, with his sights set on becoming a concert pianist. My mom was brilliant academically—she had been valedictorian of her high school class, with the added distinction of carrying the highest grade point average (nothing but As) of all the students in the Buffalo school system throughout her entire education. She would go on to excel in college, both as an undergrad and while getting her master's degree.

My parents met their first year in college. Mom was singing in the choir, and Dad was the accompanist for the Christmas concert. After one particular practice, all the girls gathered around the piano while my dad played a few bars of various songs, challenging the girls to "name that tune." He began with popular melodies, which were readily guessed. But then he decided to throw in something classical—an obscure piece by Chopin called "Revolutionary Étude"—to stump the group. His plan to outwit the girls almost worked, but with her rich classical music background, my mom recognized the piece immediately. Dad couldn't help but be impressed.

The two started talking and discovered how much they had in common. My dad had been a child prodigy on the piano, while my mom's father, William Monteith, who played tuba in the Buffalo Philharmonic Orchestra, was gifted with natural musical talent and taught himself to play nine instruments. Mom and Dad began to spend more time together, and before too long they fell in love and got married. When my brother, Barry, was born, Dad dropped out of school and began working as a security guard at the Trico factory, where windshield wipers were made. Three years later my sister, Barbara, came along. And while she was still a toddler, I arrived on June 2, 1958.

At this point my dad was still working at Trico. I remember thinking his uniform was cool because it made him look like a policeman. But it wasn't long before my parents launched their own small business directly tied to their passion for music.

My dad had learned how to tune pianos and was making extra money by working part-time for other people. With his skill in demand, it made perfect sense for my parents to start their own business. They began buying old pianos for next to nothing, then restoring and reselling them. Every instrument was perfectly tuned, fitted with new keys and strings, and refinished until the cosmetic flaws vanished. Before long, they had more pianos than space to work on them. They opened a small storefront called Roger's Quality Pianos and Organs, located on Main Street in Buffalo. Dad's uniform was now a suit and tie, and he slicked his hair back with Brylcreem. I wanted to be just like my dad, so I insisted on wearing a suit to kindergarten every day. Eventually, the kindergarten teacher called my mom.

"Mrs. Pfohl, it's really difficult for the class to finger paint when Larry is always wearing a suit." By first grade, I had outgrown my suit phase.

■ ■ ■

My parents' enterprise grew rapidly as satisfied customers spread the word. Soon everything was moved to a bigger space across the street. Mom and Dad made a dynamic team. I believe that their honesty and integrity fueled their success. And it certainly helped that my dad could play—the pianos practically walked out the door after he sat down and touched the keys. It didn't matter whether it was an upright, spinet, or concert grand; the sound he created was magical and profitable.

When business picked up, Dad added Sunday hours—now the store was open seven days a week. Before the store opened on weekends, Barry, Barbara, and I had various tasks to complete. As the youngest, I mopped the floors, cleaned the windows and bathroom, and dusted the pianos and organs. After my dad paid me for a job well done, I'd celebrate with a lunch of a burger, fries, and a vanilla milk shake at Charlie's, the soda fountain across the street. On other occasions, I'd stroll over to the drugstore next door and pick up the latest Superman comic book and all the candy my remaining money would buy. (I've always loved my sweets.)

The store required a lot of my parents' time, so after school we kids were left on our own until Mom came home to make dinner. I took full advantage of that liberty. My brother and sister were probably supposed to keep an eye on me, but they were doing their own thing with their friends. I'd get home from grade school, change clothes, search for something to eat, then head out to explore for the rest of the afternoon—free as a bird.

The neighborhood we lived in looked like the opening scene of the movie *Rudy*—lots of concrete, chain-link fences, and a plaza with a Woolworth's, a barbershop, a drugstore, and other places to hang out. I became a regular there. The more I was on my own, the happier I was. I liked being able to do what I wanted, when I wanted.

But because I came from a musically talented family, there were still expectations placed on me. All of us kids took piano lessons. Barry began with piano then switched to guitar, while Barbara became accomplished at the keyboard and also sang. But me? It was like being marched to my execution when the piano teacher, Mrs. Feldmann, came to our house once a week.

I was ten years old and determined to make my piano lessons miserable for everyone. I vowed to wear down my teacher—and my parents—until they all backed down and surrendered to my demands. Mrs. Feldmann was old. I figured she was probably born when dinosaurs were alive. She wore thick glasses and smelled like mothballs. I scooted as far away from her on the bench as I could, trying not to fall off the end.

In hindsight, I have to give Mrs. Feldmann credit. She patiently encouraged me, going over the same things, week after week. "C'mon, Larry," she'd say. "Be patient, and you'll see some progress. Just stay with it. Let's begin again."

Bam! Bam! Bam!

I banged the keys violently and screamed, "Leave me alone. I hate this!" My outbursts must have pierced my mother's heart as she waited for the half-hour lesson to be over, embarrassed at my behavior and stunned by my declaration. But it was true. I hated anything I didn't excel at, and I was terrible at playing piano. What did I need piano lessons for? Were they going to help me run faster or jump higher? That's all that mattered to me.

■ ■ ■

One day in third-grade gym class, my athletic abilities became public. We lined up by grades, five or six kids per heat, on the pavement behind the school for five different fitness activities. I took off like a shot in the fifty-yard dash, my closest competitor twenty yards behind me. I'll never forget the look on my gym teacher's face when I finished. His mouth had dropped open, his eyes riveted on his stopwatch. *Something must have happened,* I thought. *Well, I'll be happy to do it again.* I got my wish.

After the second heat, my teacher went over to the table where the official times were being recorded. A few minutes later, I learned why everyone was so excited: my time had blown the competition away—breaking the school record for the third grade and beating out all the fourth and fifth graders as well. I knew I was fast, but I had no idea I was *that* fast. I marveled at my ability and how easy it was for me.

Not only did I have lightning speed, I soared over the high jump—breaking the third-grade school record handily. I excelled in every fitness test, scoring above 100 percent across the board. My playground cred skyrocketed; everyone began treating me differently. I often heard my closest friends defending me to older kids.

"Larry is the fastest kid in the whole school, and he's only in the third grade." "Yeah, and he can jump the highest too!"

I would smile like a king, holding court while sitting on the monkey bars at recess, showing off my skills from time to time. *I really am talented. Different from the rest of my family, but still the best at what I do.*

My parents' reaction to my achievements didn't surprise me. Sports was foreign territory to them, light-years away from their world of music and art. They were happy for me, but with no point of reference, it seemed to me that the significance of my abilities was lost on them. That was okay. My natural talent didn't match any of my family's. But I was exceptional at something, and I'd stand out on my own.

During the 1968 Summer Olympics in Mexico City, I was glued to the TV. I loved every minute of it, especially the track-and-field events. My parents were at the store during most of the two-week broadcast, but my brother and sister would occasionally watch with me.

We were together when Bob Beamon obliterated the world long jump record with a distance of 29 feet 2-½ inches, so far that it exceeded the optical measuring device. People called it the "Leap of the Century," convinced it would stand until the millennium. When Beamon collapsed on the track after hearing his final distance, I sprang off the couch and announced to my siblings, "I'm going to break his world record someday!"

But that wasn't the only record I wanted to break. I concentrated on every stride that American runners Tommie Smith and John Carlos took in the 200-meter sprint. When they raised their black-gloved fists to the sky as our national anthem was played, I didn't realize what it meant or what all the fuss was about afterward. I simply admired how fast they ran and wanted to break their records too.

So I ran and ran and jumped and jumped, an enjoyable regimen. If anyone asked me what I was doing, I would quickly reply: "Training."

I didn't get a pass from playing music, though. In the next year, the piano lessons had been abandoned, but Grandpa Monteith attempted to teach me to play the trombone for band. I flat-out refused to practice but was still expected to play in a school parade when I was in fourth grade. I couldn't play a single note of the songs, but I had an ingenious plan.

Watching the musicians on either side of me, I raised my trombone, pressed my lips against the mouthpiece, puffed out my cheeks, and moved the brass slide. March, puff, slide—perfectly synchronized. I smiled to myself. *I'm good.* No one was the wiser. My "Milli Vanilli" performance would have fooled even my grandfather if he had been there.

■ ■ ■

At school, I enjoyed the sports in gym class but never chose to play on any organized team in the summer like most of my classmates. I was so focused on my track-and-field goals that I became oblivious to most other sports. One day in sixth grade I happened to see some boys shooting hoops in the neighborhood. *Looks like fun and pretty easy. I can do that.* So I asked if I could try a few shots. I dribbled a few times to get a feel for the ball. I didn't make any baskets on my first attempts, but I was hooked. From that point on, I spent hours at my friends' houses playing basketball. It made sense to switch to an indoor sport because Buffalo winters are cold, and it's hard to run in the snow and ice. I played basketball in an after-school recreation league. By the end of the season, I had proved myself to be one of the best players, if not the best.

I asked my parents for a basketball hoop at home so I could practice anytime. At first my dad said no, but he eventually came around. I would shoot for hours and never tire of it. Sometimes my brother would join me in a lively game. A good athlete, Barry could give me a workout. Inside the house, I worked on perfecting my vertical leap, aggravating my mother when she'd find fresh smudge marks from my hands on the white ceiling.

Fortunately, there was always a pickup game going on somewhere nearby. And being good at sports made it easier for me to make friends when we moved to a new neighborhood in Buffalo. As my parents' business grew, my dad relocated us several times. As soon as kids found out what I could do, everyone wanted me to be on their team.

Being good at sports really expanded my influence. I could rally kids around me to do just about anything I asked them to do—good or bad.

■ ■ ■

The shoplifting started small—a few things pocketed here and there at the mall. My middle school friends and I hung out there a lot. We'd spend hours in the stores, trying on the newest athletic wear, jewelry, and clothes. The first time I successfully swiped a pair of Converse tennis shoes (this was before security scanners at store exits), I was pumped. The thrill of defying the authorities, especially pulling off something right under their noses, was exhilarating. Before long, we were taking orders from our classmates, stealing the merchandise, and selling it. To us, it was a game.

This went on for weeks. One night, a friend and I were caught. After the security guard called my friend's parents, I gave him the number for my parents' store.

"I have your son in my office. He was caught stealing," the guard said into the phone. "Would you like to come get him?"

The guard seemed taken aback by the response. He hung up the phone and looked at me. "He said to lock you up and throw away the key."

"You must have talked to my dad," I said. "Call back and ask for my mom."

Fortunately for me, the mall didn't file charges, believing it was my first offense. My mom eventually picked me up, barely saying a word to me. When we got home, I immediately went to my room. I heard Dad come home later that evening and braced myself for a beating with his belt. "Lawrence, I'm beyond disappointed with you," he said. "I don't even recognize you as my son. No son of mine would steal something that wasn't his. I didn't raise my children that way."

His words were chilling and hurt me more than any physical punishment from him. I was grounded for a month.

My parents seemed stunned by this latest development and probably wondered where my total disregard for everything they had taught me came from. Were sports to blame? The people I hung out with?

■ ■ ■

My passion for sports seemed to remain a mystery to my parents. Initially, I think they liked the idea of me being supervised by adults in some activity, but it was still a challenge to get them to agree to everything I asked. When I entered ninth grade, my friends convinced me to go out for football in the fall. Since I wanted to spend time with my friends, I brought home the parental permission slip for my dad to sign. He refused.

"That isn't a sport! They're like gladiators out there. What's sporting about putting on pads and running into other people? What good could possibly come of that?"

I knew he didn't want any feedback from me. When Dad spoke, we all listened. Everything was pretty much black-and-white for him; he was serious about everything, including my name. Everybody called me "Lar," including my mom and siblings. It made perfect sense to my father why he never used it.

"Look at your birth certificate," Dad would explain. "I did not name you Lar, and I did not name you Larry. I named you Lawrence. That's the name we chose for you." To this day, I'm Lawrence to him— always have been, always will be.

I forged my dad's name on the permission slip. For a while, he didn't even know I was playing, but my mom did. She tried to come to as many of my games as possible when she could get away from the store.

2
AN ATTITUDE IN THE MAKING

I began goofing off with a J. C. Penney plastic weight set at home, not knowing what I was doing. I had always loved doing push-ups, so I was already more muscular than most other kids my age. I just hadn't realized how physically developed I was becoming.

But other people were definitely noticing.

The summer after my freshman year of high school, we moved into a new house. My parents hired me to paint its exterior as a summer job. I had "apprenticed" for years under Grandpa Monteith, who supplemented his income as a musician and artist by painting houses. A few times my brother and dad grabbed brushes and helped, but I did the majority of the labor. It was a sultry summer, so I often worked shirtless. As the weeks passed, my tan got darker and my blond hair got lighter. Soon I became the subject of neighborhood gossip, especially since we were still getting to know everyone.

Finally, someone said to my mom, "Where did you find that Adonis to paint your house?"

"Oh, him?" she laughed. "That's my youngest son, Larry. He'll be a sophomore in high school this fall."

"He's in high school?" the woman said, completely flabbergasted.

■ ■ ■

It wasn't only my body that was getting larger. My attitude was growing too. If someone challenged me—in sports or otherwise—I didn't back down.

That included Carlos Garcia.

Garcia was a senior and a Golden Gloves boxer. He was also the leader of "The Motor Heads," industrial arts students who spent most of their time in the school's shop, working on cars and learning other skilled trades. They were adversaries of the college-bound athletes like me, but we usually kept our distance from each other.

One Friday night I was with my buddies when we ran into a group of Motor Heads. One of them began mouthing off to me. It was too dark to see who it was, and my friends held me back from going after him. Still, I wasn't about to let it slide. My anger built all weekend.

First thing on Monday morning, an informant pointed out my challenger. I pinned him against the wall, grabbed him by the throat, and threw him down on the floor. "If you want to play the 'big man,' let's settle this after school."

Apparently, the Motor Heads talked about me all morning, because at lunchtime, I was surprised when one of them approached me in the cafeteria, surrounded by his henchmen. "If you want to fight someone, meet me after school."

I didn't know who this kid was, but with the buzz in the cafeteria, it seemed everyone else did, including my friends. "That's Carlos Garcia, a Golden Gloves boxer. Are you really going to fight him?"

It was crazy, but there was no backing out now.

It was hard to concentrate for the rest of the afternoon. I knew I was strong, but I didn't know how I would fare against a trained boxer. My adrenaline was pumping, and butterflies were fluttering in my stomach. The details of the showdown spread quickly throughout the school. I got nods and words of encouragement as well as deadly stares. Amazingly, despite all of the excited whispering, none of the teachers knew what was going on.

As soon as school let out, a huge crowd began to form in the soccer field between the high school and middle school. I couldn't believe how many kids were there. The main athletes and Motor Heads pushed their way up front to control the chaos, forming a small circle. Hundreds of kids pressed in behind them, shouting and jumping up and down, trying to catch a glimpse of the action. Little did I know that the scene would be a harbinger of my future.

The crowd's anticipation was palpable. As Garcia and I began sizing each other up like two prized bulls, the shouting died down. Everyone seemed to be holding their breath.

I was waiting for him to take his first swing; my strategy was to duck under, tackle him, and get him on the ground. I was so focused, I couldn't hear the crowd. Suddenly, my opportunity came. I took Mr. Motor Head down to the ground and began beating him in the face with my fists and elbows. It was over in less than a minute.

After pulling me off Garcia, my friends jumped around me and raised my arm in victory. I couldn't believe how easy it had been. A police car pulled up, and the crowd scattered. I went back into the school to get ready for basketball practice, but Garcia followed me and got in my face again.

Some teachers intervened. One look at Garcia's swollen face tipped them off that they had missed the main event. Our reward was a suspension.

A few weeks later, Garcia attempted a surprise attack in the cafeteria, trying to get his reputation back. I couldn't take the bait. I was on the basketball team, and if I got one more suspension, I would be kicked off the team. Finally, he gave up and left me alone.

Now there was no doubt I was "the Man" of Orchard Park High School.

■ ■ ■

It wasn't just students like Carlos Garcia whose authority I would challenge. I began defying teachers so often that I wore a path to the principal's office. I tallied up numerous suspensions during high school, but never enough in succession to affect my ability to play sports. My conduct was bewildering to my parents.

One day during my senior year I was feeling more raucous than usual as I angrily pounded on the door of the weight room adjacent to the gym. Behind the locked door was a brand-new Universal weight station, the most advanced equipment available at the time. And yet we athletes had only limited access. That did not sit well with me. I voiced my opinion loudly in the hallway, which caused the assistant principal to come out of his office.

As a former football player, the assistant principal always intimidated people by his size alone. He heard the commotion and pushed through the crowd until he found me. "Break it up—now!"

"What have I done? I have a right to speak my mind. It's not my fault that everyone is listening."

He glared at me. This guy was used to students backing down. *Not this time. Not with me.*

"We have every right to use this weight room at any time!" I addressed the growing crowd gathered around me. "Can you believe this? It's unfair and a waste of our parents' hard-earned taxpayer dollars!"

"Move on, Pfohl," he growled.

I refused to budge. Within seconds, the assistant principal and I were nose to nose, with fists clenched, about to take a swing at each other. I wasn't intimidated and was ready to go at it before other faculty members arrived and quickly separated us. I earned another three-day suspension.

■ ■ ■

Basketball had been my first love since middle school. When the NBA introduced a new Buffalo franchise in 1970, Barry and I were regulars at the Braves games, whooping loudly when Bob McAdoo lit up the scoreboard. He was my new inspiration, and my Olympic dreams of track stardom were replaced by hopes of an exceptional college basketball career, Olympic team gold, then on to the NBA.

By the time I was a freshman, I was pulling off some highlight-reel slams in practice without any trouble at all. I had trained myself to dunk, starting with a baseball, then moving on to a softball, a volleyball, and finally a basketball. Unfortunately, I could never show off my skills in an actual game—dunking was prohibited in high school basketball at the time. In my sophomore year, I was the starting power forward for the varsity team.

For three summers in a row, I attended the Five-Star Basketball Camps for elite players, comparable to the Nike Basketball Camps and Adidas Phenom America Camps held today. More than once I was asked if I played football; my body type looked more tailored to football than basketball. But for me, high school football was all about hanging out with my friends and killing time before basketball season began. My coach, Harris Weinke, thought differently, believing that I had unlimited potential. Because of my athletic ability, I played tailback, fullback, tight end, linebacker, offensive guard, defensive end, and on special teams. I went both ways and did well in almost every position.

Yet I still thought basketball was going to be my ticket to fame and fortune. And then reality hit—I had stopped growing at six feet four inches. I could dominate the boards on the high school court because I had huge ups—anywhere from a 36- to 38-inch vertical leap. In practice, I would show off by throwing down a two-handed tomahawk dunk from a standstill position under the hoop. With a running start, I could get my hand over the top of the painted square on the backboard. Impressive for sure, but the reality was that I would probably need to switch positions to play in the big-time conferences.

Although I was still focused on pursuing college hoops, Coach Weinke heard the rumor that I wasn't going to play football my senior year. He called me into his office and said, "If you focused on football with the same passion you have for basketball, you'd be a shoo-in for a Division I scholarship."

It might have been the best advice I ever received, as college scouts soon came to know who I was.

■ ■ ■

Compared to New Jersey, Pennsylvania, and Ohio, our part of the country had never really been considered a fertile recruiting ground for Division I college teams. However, my senior class had an unusual collection of athletic talent, luring representatives from almost all of the major college programs. Like bees in a hive, they were buzzing aplenty about two of my blue-chip teammates: future longtime NFL starters Craig Wolfley and Jim Burt, who was a year younger.

Wolfley was a dominant offensive lineman who would eventually start at Syracuse as a freshman, before going on to play twelve seasons in the NFL, most of which were spent with the Pittsburgh Steelers. Burt was a tough-minded nose tackle who later played with me again at the University of Miami before making the most of his eleven years in the NFL, contributing to two Super Bowl winning teams—the 1986 New York Giants and the 1989 San Francisco 49ers.

When the college coaches came to look at my teammates, they couldn't help but see me on the films too. Even though I hadn't officially been on anyone's radar, they weren't going to leave without meeting me. My name was added to their priority list.

The Orchard Park Quakers did well my final year, and the major college coaches were all taking notice. By season's end, I was up to 235 pounds and could run the forty-yard dash in 4.6 seconds—a perfect combination for football.

With football season over, I got ready for basketball. The schools that had expressed keen interest in me for my football talent continued to pursue me, inviting me for weekend recruiting trips, leading up to the National Signing Day in February. I had torn a ligament in the thumb of my shooting hand during a passing drill right before Christmas. Since I couldn't play basketball while I was injured, it was perfect timing to attend the football recruiting trips. In the winter of my senior year, I narrowed my schools down to five NCAA campuses, all on the East Coast—Penn State, Boston College, Wake Forest, Annapolis, and the University of Miami. I was treated royally everywhere, and each school had something unique to offer. It was nice to have options.

Penn State was a football powerhouse that churned out NFL-bound players year after year, but I liked the coaching staff at Boston College. Wake Forest had a small campus and was superb academically. The US Naval Academy at Annapolis attracted me because the idea of becoming a navy pilot appealed to my penchant for speed and could ultimately lead to a career as a commercial pilot.

Annapolis was definitely my dad's choice. During our visit, we had been guests at a formal dinner served by uniformed midshipmen decked out in white gloves. My dad was very impressed.

Finally, there was Miami, with its balmy weather, even in winter. That was a no-brainer to someone from Buffalo.

■ ■ ■

The night before the big collegiate decision, I was floored when Joe Paterno showed up at my high school basketball game to see me.

My parents and I had met him during my official visit to Penn State. They had eaten dinner at Coach Paterno's house along with the parents of other recruits who were on campus that weekend.

I was finally getting back on the court after my injury when Coach Paterno decided to visit. He sat with my parents in the stands, causing quite a hubbub. He had never personally come to western New York to see anyone, and now he was coming to *my* house after the game to make his final pitch for the Nittany Lions. If the head guy was that interested, maybe I was supposed to go to Penn State after all.

To say the least, it was an interesting evening with my parents and the coach. "You have an extremely talented son, Mr. and Mrs. Pfohl," he said. "Every one of his high school coaches says he's a hard worker and always gives 110 percent. It's a rare athlete who can play as many positions as well as he has. He would be a boon to us, and we'd prepare him for a successful future."

My mom steered the conversation to academics, emphasizing that my future success would be determined there. I had clearly inherited my smarts from my parents, easily maintaining a 92 average throughout high school, enough to keep my parents from yanking me out of sports.

"Penn State is a prestigious academic university with an outstanding faculty," the coach said, changing tactics immediately. "Our graduates excel in every field they enter, and we look after our athletes. Lawrence has the grades to go far in whatever he pursues."

My parents continued to ask questions about everything except sports. When Coach Paterno got up to leave, he asked my parents if they wanted to join him for a picture.

"No thanks," my dad said politely. Maybe the coach found the lack of fawning on the part of my parents refreshing. Probably he was shocked. I imagine it was the first time he had ever been turned down for a photo op. I jumped on the awkward moment, saying, "Sure,

I'll get a picture with you," just to make him feel better. We posed in front of the fireplace. When he left, my parents and I continued talking. My decision was made. That night I started thinking about how I'd look in Penn State navy blue and white.

But I still had one more unforgettable event left in my senior year.

■ ■ ■

I could definitely get a party started. Even though I was underage, getting beer was never a problem because my physical size fooled everyone. Wearing my Buffalo Bills sweatpants and T-shirt, I'd drive to the local Kmart and pick up a six-pack without being asked to show my ID. As I checked out, the cashier would often ask, "What position do you play?"

"Linebacker."

It wasn't a lie; I did play linebacker—for my high school team. The fact that I was often mistaken for a pro football player impressed my friends. We never drank to get drunk; just two or three beers each to get a little buzz. When we were really bored, we'd add some shooters like Bacardi 151 blue flamers. Light 'em up and drink 'em. And while we drank, I'd come up with another brilliant way to get in trouble.

In one particular Buffalo neighborhood, residents competed against one another for the honor of owning the most distinctive handmade wooden mailbox. In March of my senior year, following an unusual ice storm that knocked out all the power, my friends and I were bored and decided it would be fun to whack as many of the mailboxes as we could with sledgehammers and axes. It would be a crowning touch to the previous acts of vandalism we had committed, such as breaking car windows and spray-painting graffiti on buildings.

My parents were out of town when we came up with the plan to assault the mailboxes. Joining me were some of my best partners in crime—my teammates from the football team. This stunt would require some brawn, and besides, breaking the law was always more exciting when I shared the experience with others.

So, with the headlights off, we went for a joyride in my dad's car—drinking, driving, and swinging away at the unsuspecting mailboxes. We had mangled dozens of them and were pulling up to the last one. It belonged to one of our classmates, who was making out with her boyfriend in the car parked in the driveway. She saw us and ran inside the house, and her parents called the police. We were pulled over within minutes.

It was a big news story because it involved me, the football team's top wide receiver, the star tailback, and two other outstanding players. We were fortunate not to be hit with federal charges of destroying government property. Since it was the first arrest for all of us, we were fined and given a nine o'clock curfew. If we broke curfew, we were going to jail. It definitely put a dent in our partying for the rest of our senior year—we missed extracurricular activities and even some of our graduation celebrations.

Fortunately, my brush with the law was minor enough not to affect my collegiate future.

3
THE OLD
COLLEGE TRY

From Buffalo, New York, to State College, Pennsylvania, is a two-hundred-mile drive. "Happy Valley" is the nickname given to Centre County, and more often to Penn State University in adjacent University Park. The school sits in the shadow of Mount Nittany. This geographic landmark welcomes every student to the beautiful campus that stretches over hundreds of acres. From the Old Main building to the limestone statue of the Nittany Lion poised for the next photograph snapped by students and visitors alike, the sprawling university has a storied history academically and athletically. What became known in 2011 regarding Jerry Sandusky, Joe Paterno, and other football staff members is undeniably tragic. The whole sordid story is very sad, and I feel for the victims and their families.

When I arrived at Penn State University in the fall of 1976, it was a culture shock to me. Since I hadn't come from a football-crazy part of the country, I was stunned by how the sport transformed quaint State College into a place overrun by rabid fans. On a fall Saturday afternoon the trees were ablaze with seasonal color, and the atmosphere was electrically charged. Beaver Stadium was packed with more than sixty thousand fans, rallied by the university Blue Band that marched down the street to the field.

My freshman class included future pros Bruce Clark, Matt Suhey, Matt Millen, and Irv Pankey, among others. I vividly remember walking into the team's weight room for the first time. I considered myself a pretty good weight lifter, with muscles to show for it. Then I saw Bruce Clark. I thought he was an NFL player who had come to give the team a pep talk. He was bench-pressing 405 for a bunch of reps. I'm sure when he introduced himself as an incoming freshman teammate, my mouth dropped open in astonishment.

The football facilities were on the far end of campus, opposite from where I was being housed. My roommate was Pete Harris, the younger brother of former Penn State star tailback and then-current NFL sensation Franco Harris of the Pittsburgh Steelers. Pete and I saw each other often when it involved football—and sometimes in our room when I was doing some cramming for a test. I had used last-minute study methods in high school and gotten As, so I figured it would work in college, too.

Who needs to study every day when you can rely on short-term memory? Academic achievement was a necessary evil. I was on campus to play football, socialize, and occasionally go to class—in that order.

I loved the sudden freedom to do whatever I wanted, whenever I wanted. No more trips to the principal's office or calls to my parents. As a college athlete, if I kept my grades up, no one checked my attendance in class. I'd find a fellow athlete or a friend who actually went to class to keep me posted on upcoming tests or papers I needed to prepare for. The only thing I had to attend, along with every other athlete, was a mandatory study hall two or three times a week.

■ ■ ■

A few weeks after arriving at Penn State, I was "studying" when a friend came up to my table and said, "Hey, I met a couple of girls. One's a cutie-pie. I asked them to stop by and visit if they'd like."

The two girls eventually came over and introduced themselves. The "cutie-pie" was Peggy Hall, a walk-on track star from nearby Unionville, Pennsylvania. I can't remember a lot about our initial meeting, other than that I was captivated by her beauty. A stunning brunette with brownish-green eyes and high cheekbones, she looked exotic. (I would later learn that her mother was Japanese.) Peggy was a middle distance runner specializing in the 800 meter, which required a combination of speed, strength, and endurance.

Surprisingly, I was pretty shy around girls. I hadn't dated very much in high school, so girls were a mystery to me. But I was immediately comfortable with Peggy because she was so easy to talk to. More than anything, I wanted to impress her. When it was time to leave, I said, "You shouldn't walk back to your dorm by yourself. Let me walk you home." I was elated when she agreed. After that first meeting, I spent most of my study halls trying to find her.

The next time we met, our conversation lasted more than a few minutes. We happened to run into each other at an off-campus party. As soon as I saw her, everything around me seemed to disappear. We found a quiet corner to talk while the party continued around us. I loved her quick wit and easygoing disposition. Time seemed to stop for us, so much so that we were surprised when the party broke up.

We hadn't really eaten, so we decided to stop at the McDonald's near campus to grab a bite to eat before I walked Peggy back to her dorm. When we sat down with our trays, I realized that I had forgotten something.

"Oh, man, I didn't grab any napkins," I said. "I'll be right back."

But Peggy jumped to her feet before I did.

"I'll get them," she said. "Just relax."

I didn't know what to say, so I just sat there quietly with a silly ear-to-ear grin plastered across my face, like some wily cat that had just raided the pantry. I was head over heels in love.

From then on, we'd sit together in study hall and I'd walk her back to her dorm afterward. Peggy's dorm was a half mile past mine, but I felt like I was walking on air every time I was with her.

Sports had always been my faithful companion before I met Peggy, but she had stolen my heart. Her love and support meant a lot to me, especially when my debut at Penn State turned out to be less than stellar.

■ ■ ■

I didn't appear in any games my first year—not an unusual situation for freshmen at most major colleges and universities. High-profile programs had budgets to stockpile athletic talent. It was extremely rare to find standout athletes like my teammates Bruce Clark and Matt Millen, who were developed enough to start right away as freshmen at a big-time school like Penn State. Most of us supported the team from the sidelines, which was fine for me.

In practice, the coaches and I locked horns on what position I was best suited to play. Penn State was Linebacker U, and with my height and speed, the coaches were determined to make me a pass-rushing defensive end or an outside linebacker.

I thought it was a terrible idea.

I had grown up idolizing the Buffalo Bills, with O. J. Simpson and his offensive line called the "Electric Company." All-pro Joe DeLamielleure and Reggie McKenzie were the star pulling guards who helped open up lanes for O. J. I had met Joe D. when he worked with our high school team during the summer. I wanted to play offensive guard and be another Joe or Reggie.

The Penn State staff tried to convince me otherwise. "Larry, you were made to be an outside linebacker. With your height, speed, pass-rushing skills, run-stopping abilities, and strength, you could be one of the greatest linebackers we've ever had."

I disagreed. I was determined to be an offensive guard, and, true to my nature, once I envisioned something, it was difficult to convince me otherwise.

Rather than listen to me complain during the season, they moved me to offensive guard on the scout team before the season started. The offensive scout team emulated the opposing offense so that our defensive starters and other key personnel wouldn't have any surprises in the upcoming game. We took our duties seriously.

In the off-season, I continued to work out—adding muscle—in anticipation of eventually getting my shot. I now weighed about 250 pounds.

■ ■ ■

A week into spring practice in 1977, I was playing offensive guard when I heard Coach Paterno call my name.

"Hey, Larry Pfohl. Get in there at noseguard."

What's going on now?

I'd never played noseguard before, and now I was in a full-speed scrimmage. I did pretty well on my first couple of plays, even going out and breaking up an attempted screen pass. On the fourth play I broke through the line of scrimmage and into the backfield. I was pleased with myself and thought, *Wow, this is easy.*

Then I heard it—a distinct growling sound. Nittany Lion offensive linemen intimidate their opponents by growling just before making contact. I was the target in a trap play. I remember turning my head and seeing a behemoth offensive lineman coming right at me, but it was too late. He went low on the outside of my left knee. The sharp pain was immediate. As I went down, I knew something was really wrong.

My spring football camp was over.

I was rushed to the hospital in nearby Harrisburg. My knee was X-rayed, and the orthopedic specialist determined that the medial collateral ligament in my left knee had been torn by the hit. Rather than immediate surgery, he advised a wait-and-see approach; once the swelling had subsided, he'd make a recommendation. I was glad not to go under the knife. My leg was put in an immobilizer, and I was on crutches for the rest of the spring.

Peggy was with me as much as possible, even when I came down with a bad case of mononucleosis. She was an attentive and caring nurse. Flat on my back from the mono, there was no way I could go to class, and my grades reflected it. I was forced to drop some courses.

In order to remain eligible for football, I had to go to summer school. I took my needed classes at Florida Atlantic University in Boca Raton, where my parents had recently moved.

■ ■ ■

While I was enjoying the sunshine and palm trees, I mulled over my experience at Penn State and decided it was time to move on. The program wasn't a good fit for me, and to be honest, the temperatures in Happy Valley my first winter had been brutal. I recalled that the recruiter I had met from Annapolis had since moved on to the University of Miami. So I contacted him and asked if the Hurricanes might be interested in me. He said he'd let me know.

I was still awaiting word when I had to report back to Penn State in August for my sophomore year. Peggy, the bright spot in my life, was the only reason I wanted to go back.

A week after I returned, I got the call from the Miami coach: the 'Canes wanted me. There was one hitch—I would have to transfer immediately. I met with my position coach at Penn State and explained the situation, saying that I wanted to be closer to my parents in South Florida. It wasn't exactly the truth, but I knew Coach

Paterno was a devoted family man and if the position coach gave that reason, it might make him sign my transfer papers more readily.

It took a couple of weeks before Penn State released me, once they were finally convinced my heart to play football there was gone.

I couldn't wait to tell Peggy. Our relationship had become serious in the months since we'd met. We were already talking about running off and getting married rather than waiting until we'd finished college.

"Why should we wait?" I'd say to her. "It's obvious we love each other. There is no one else I want to spend the rest of my life with except you." Peggy felt the same way. I hadn't formally proposed and we hadn't looked for rings, but it was a given that we were going to marry in the near future. Twelve hundred miles between us wouldn't change anything. Peggy promised she would join me as quickly as she could. But as soon as I left, Peggy's family, her friends, and her track coach began to talk her out of it.

"How well do you really know this guy?" her coach asked. "Are you sure this is what you want to do?"

I believe the coach was more worried about how Peggy's absence would affect his track team than about her happiness. She was a key leg on the Nittany Lions 4 x 800-meter relay team that had reached nationals the year before. He didn't want to lose her. And he knew that it would be the end of her collegiate track career—Miami didn't have a program to transfer to.

Peggy's family had their doubts as well, and they advised her not to rush into marriage. Everyone's persistence finally wore her down. Peggy was apologetic and tearful on the phone when she broke the news to me: she wanted to slow things down. I was initially stunned by her unexpected change of heart, but that surprise soon turned into deep disappointment.

I wasn't used to not getting what I wanted, but I eventually pulled myself together. We agreed to make the long-distance relationship work. We'd call each other several times a week, and I anxiously awaited the end of the season, when I could visit her over Christmas break.

■ ■ ■

The contrast between Sunshine U and Happy Valley was day and night. Where Penn State had been full of rolling hills and forests, Miami was sand and palm trees.

One of the hot spots for students was the quadruple-size swimming pool with an adjacent smoothie bar at the heart of the campus. Girls would wear sarongs over their bikinis to class. It was surreal, to say the least.

The focal point for me was the athletes' cafeteria. From 6 a.m. to 10 p.m., we could go there and order whatever we wanted to eat—a training table extraordinaire.

I was housed in a coed dorm, sharing a room with another football player. Neither of us was interested in going to class. There were way too many other, more fun, things to do.

When I arrived on campus, I picked up a bundle of books for my classes. I never opened them. It was a Miami football tradition to not "break the seal" on any textbooks. I'm not sure how such a wretched "tradition" ever began or if it's around anymore today, but it was expected when I attended The U.

As far as interior decorating, we put tinfoil on the inside of our dorm-room windows, closed the hurricane shutters, and then turned the thermostat down to fifty-five degrees, making it like an icebox inside. For us big guys, it was an ideal temperature for sleeping; we were like hibernating bears. We'd stay up until the wee hours of the night, crawl under the covers, wake up at noon to grab lunch, then head off to practice. The daily routine worked perfectly for me; I was practicing with the team but was redshirted, ineligible to play for another year because of the NCAA rule on transfers.

On the days when we did get out of bed early, we'd head over to Crandon Park Beach in nearby Key Biscayne, which was *the* hot beach back then. We'd spend the day there, making it back in time for practice.

With so much going on, who had time to worry about school?

Because we weren't opening our books or going to class, we concocted a plan to cheat on tests. It became a game to outwit our professors, who were always trying to catch us. But we had devised elaborate and creative systems of cheating that utilized the help of the Hurricane Honeys—female students who showed visiting recruits around campus—as well as other coconspirators.

Our deception worked, but I have often thought that if we had spent half as much time studying as we did preparing ways to cheat, we'd have all gotten As.

■ ■ ■

Of course, we made time for a social life, too. On Friday nights during the off-season, we'd load our cars with girls and drive to Big Daddy's, the local hot spot whose "Drink and Drown" night was a big draw for students. We could drink all we wanted fairly inexpensively, and we usually got pretty hammered.

One night, after drinking at Big Daddy's, we started talking about the rich kids at school with their luxury cars that their parents had bought them. "They drive around in their Mercedes and BMWs, trying to look cool in their Ray-Bans. Let's have a little fun with them."

We parked down the street from a number of sports cars, grabbed the beer cans we had been drinking, and began stacking them on the hoods.

"C'mon, I have a better idea. Follow me." I scrambled on the roof of a Mercedes and began jumping up and down. A few of my buddies joined me. With two or three of us jumping simultaneously, we could stomp the roofs of the cars down to the seats.

We didn't consider how much destruction we were leaving behind; it was too much fun while we were doing it. Over the next few weeks, we changed the game and started flipping cars on their roofs; it took us only about fifteen seconds per car. When we finally got bored and stopped, we had damaged half a dozen cars without getting caught.

For all the goofing off we did, when it was time for spring football, I was ready to get down to business.

■ ■ ■

By the spring of 1978, I had grown to 270 pounds, and following a great spring practice I earned the starting position at right guard. Coach Lou Saban and his staff loved what they saw and soon began touting me as the next great football player to hail from the program.

A Dallas Cowboys scout who attended our practices pulled me aside one day. "Keep working hard," he advised me, "and you'll be a surefire NFL first-round pick." I appreciated his words of encouragement, which fueled my drive. College was a stepping-stone to the pros for me, and I was confident I'd make it.

Miami wasn't the national powerhouse that it would become a couple of years later, but it was definitely a program on the rise. My future on the gridiron was looking bright. I went home to Buffalo that summer since my parents had moved back.

When I returned to Miami that fall, I shared an on-campus apartment with two teammates—Tony Galente and Jim Burt, who had played high school ball with me. The three of us together were a volatile mix, and one evening a memorable escapade escalated into complete madness.

That night Jim got into a fight on the telephone with his girlfriend from back home. Just a few weeks into the football season, Peggy and I had broken up over the phone, and I was still fuming. Tony was having girlfriend problems too.

Suddenly, Jim picked up his brand-new TV and hurled it to the floor, smashing it to pieces. Tony and I looked at each other for a second, then joined the mayhem.

We went on a rampage, trashing everything in sight. We ripped out the built-in bookshelves, the bathroom sink, and the toilet. In about three minutes, it looked like a hurricane had blown through.

Just then, we heard someone banging at the front door. Burt darted to the bathroom and somehow squeezed his big body through the small window and scurried away into the night. Tony fled out of a back bedroom window. I went to the door and looked through the peephole. It was the resident assistant, a former football player, who identified himself and told me to open the door.

"I've called the police!" the RA shouted.

Maybe leaving is a good plan after all.

I hopped out the same window Tony had and nearly fell into the arms of the RA. It was dark out, and my size was intimidating enough that he didn't say a word, so I just turned and walked away. That night I stayed at my brother's apartment to establish an alibi. I knew I would need it when I faced Coach Saban.

The following day all three of us were called to his office. Unfortunately for us, after he had been awakened in the middle of the night and told what had happened, he came over to the scene of the crime and saw the damage with his own two eyes. He was furious.

Tony, Jim, and I each looked Coach Saban dead in the eye and lied. I spoke first. "It wasn't us, Coach. Somebody else got into our apartment when we weren't there and destroyed it. I was in Fort Lauderdale last night." Tony and Jim each said they had been with their respective girlfriends.

I doubt there's any way Coach Saban believed us, but he also couldn't completely prove we were responsible for the damage, either. Only four games into the season, I'm sure he was reluctant to suspend three of his starters.

That should have been the end of it. We should have been on our best behavior from that point on, grateful to still be on the team after getting away with all we'd done.

But that wasn't the case.

■ ■ ■

A week later, the team traveled to Atlanta to play Georgia Tech. It was Friday, October 13, 1978, and we had checked into the Peachtree Hotel downtown.

I was dressed and ready to go to the team meeting when Tony doused me with a bucket of ice water. I was infuriated. Lacking a change of clothes, I decided to skip the meeting and seek revenge. I went to the front desk, pretended to be Tony, said I had misplaced my key, and got a duplicate key to his room. Once inside, I went crazy, spraying shaving cream on the walls and the bed linens and throwing water everywhere. It wasn't nearly as destructive as the apartment incident, but it was still a big mess. The next day the team lost to Georgia Tech 24–19.

First thing on Monday morning, Tony and I were summoned to Coach Saban's office. "What is wrong with you?" he yelled. "First the apartment, now this? There is no excuse for this kind of behavior, especially on the road. You've embarrassed all of us."

Coach seemed to be putting all the blame on Tony, and as soon as he started mentioning a suspension, I jumped in, explaining how things had happened. I thought maybe he'd admire me for standing up and taking the fall. But his reaction was the exact opposite.

"You're off the team!"

What? I couldn't believe my ears. *I don't deserve such a severe punishment.*

It was a hard thing to swallow. Coach was using me to send a message to the rest of the team: this is unacceptable behavior for a Miami athlete, no matter how talented you are.

When we left his office, Coach Saban called my mom to let her know that I had been kicked off the team, but not out of school. He hoped I would improve my grades and start behaving like a civilized young man.

All I could think of was what had been taken away from me. I couldn't eat with the rest of the players anymore; I was relegated to eating in the student cafeteria. And I was prohibited from using the athletes' training room to work out with my friends. I was already so far behind in my classes that school seemed like a waste of time. So I impulsively marched into the registrar's office that same day and promptly withdrew from the university.

I called my mom to let her know I had been kicked off the team, but I didn't tell her I had withdrawn from school. I wasn't really in the mood to see my parents just yet, so I called Barry.

"Can I stay at your place?" I asked. Thankfully, my brother said I was welcome to stay as long as I wanted.

Of course, my parents found out the whole story soon enough. When the registrar's office notified Coach Saban of what I had done, he had a staff member call my parents in hopes of tracking me down and reasoning with me.

A newspaper reporter had discovered my whereabouts and did a phone interview with me about what had transpired. If I hadn't been such a highly touted player for the Hurricanes, it probably wouldn't have been a big story. But my star had been rising, so this was juicy news. I didn't hold back. I blasted Coach Saban and the entire Hurricanes program in the newspaper, effectively killing any chance I might have had of ever returning to Miami.

In a matter of minutes, I'd slammed the door on my collegiate football career.

4
A COLORFUL GROUP OF FRIENDS

When one door closes, you head to the next available one. For me, it was literally a door.

Because of the league's rules, I wouldn't be eligible for the NFL Draft for two years, so in the meantime I needed to find a job. Ideally, I wanted something that didn't interfere with my daily workouts at Gold's Gym. The Gold's Gym franchise really was the mecca for physical fitness in the late 1970s, the place where everyone came to see and be seen. This was the era when bodybuilding became more mainstream, fueled by *Pumping Iron*, the docudrama starring Arnold Schwarzenegger and Lou Ferrigno. I loved the movie when it came out and read subsequent books like *Arnold's Bodybuilding for Men*.

When I was a student at Miami, I had picked up extra money as a part-time greeter at a local club. I had enjoyed being part of the nightclub scene—it had been fast cash and *usually* problem free. But you had to be ready for the unexpected every night—it was part of the job description.

I ended up working at two of the most popular clubs in Fort Lauderdale: Pete and Lenny's and Mr. Pip's. The managers were impressed that I came with experience from a high-end Miami club, one that Joe Namath frequented, so they both hired me. I began working every night, alternating between the two locations. I appreciated that the hours fit nicely into my schedule of dedicated time at the gym, which I continued in hopes of that NFL berth.

I worked the front door at both clubs. The owners liked the fact that I looked imposing and yet was articulate. As with any business, first impressions at a nightclub mean a lot, and I was the first person a customer would see. No one could mistake me for a thug. There were times when all of us—me working the door and the bouncers inside the club—had to muscle a few rowdies, but more often we could reason with people and prevent trouble before it started. We let guests know that if they had any plans of causing a problem, our club wasn't the place to do it. Night after night, there were people lined up for blocks trying to get inside.

I liked being the greeter/doorman because it fit my personality. After a few months, I decided to work only at Pete and Lenny's; it was more upscale than Mr. Pip's, with live bands and a plush atmosphere. I was the manager's right-hand man and the owner's bodyguard at the front door.

The drug trade was flourishing in South Florida in the late '70s to early '80s, and the club scene attracted some of the biggest local dealers. Everybody knew them. They were all ethnicities and colors: Cuban, Hispanic, Black, Caucasian. The dealers flaunted their wealth and pulled up in Lamborghinis, Ferraris, or stretch limousines. It was like a red-carpet scene every night, as the men strutted into the club wearing flashy leisure suits or sports jackets with lapels big enough to land a plane on. Their shirts were usually unbuttoned to mid-chest to show off a Fort Knox of gold jewelry. On their arms were stunning women with big hair who shimmered in their sequins and iridescent miniskirts, ready to dance in four-inch platform shoes with eight-inch spike heels. Walking was a little precarious for many; invariably someone would fall down inside the doorway, so I started automatically saying, "Watch your step, please."

As you might expect, the drug dealers never wanted to wait in line. They'd make their way up to the front with their entourages. They'd greet me with "How ya doin' tonight?" and coolly slip me a hundred dollar bill in a handshake. Either on the way in or on the way out, I was paid for giving them preferential treatment.

It wasn't unusual for me to pocket up to a thousand dollars a night. At the end of my shift, I'd divide my front-door take with the other bouncers working inside. That was the club policy, and I agreed with it. They had to endure the smoke and the pounding music, both of which gave me a headache.

Being the greeter at *the* most popular club in Fort Lauderdale does attract an interesting group of friends. The drug dealers weren't the only distinctive regulars at the club. It was also a late-night hangout for members of the Mafia. All of us at the club knew that these guys were high up in some of the most powerful Mob families in the country. No one mentioned what families they were part of or what their titles were within the organizations. Everything was handled discreetly. Quite honestly, I figured it was probably best to *not* know much about them. What they did outside of the club didn't concern me. My job was to treat them with respect while they were there.

Just like the drug dealers, the mafiosi arrived in high style. They didn't dress quite as ostentatiously, but their attire was expensive and impeccably tailored. Each night at the door, we'd exchange pleasantries. They seemed concerned about my well-being and always asked if I needed anything. I felt their interest was genuine and kept thinking that it was nice to know that there were people outside my family who really cared about me.

As we got to know each other, they started inviting me out to eat when the club closed at 4 a.m. We'd go to a local twenty-four-hour diner to unwind, one that served up great home fries and vanilla milk shakes.

One of the guys took a special liking to me. One night, he asked me if I'd be interested in house-sitting at his place while he was in New York. He came to Florida for only a few days each month.

"I need someone I can trust to keep an eye on the house," he said. "I'll leave the keys to the Lamborghini and the Ferrari and the cigarette boat. You can bring your friends over if you want to. Essentially, my house is yours. You just need to make sure the cleaning staff is doing what I'm paying them to do. Other than that, my colleagues and I would like you to meet us at the airport when I get back in town. How does a grand a week sound?"

Hang out at his ritzy house for a grand a week? A lot of NFL players weren't making that kind of money back then.

It was extremely tempting. From our conversations in the diner, they all knew I was crashing at both my parents' home and my brother's apartment to save money. The other two men at the table sat quietly, undoubtedly taking mental notes of my reaction to this generous proposition.

I seriously considered the offer before getting back to him a few days later with my answer.

"Thank you, sir, for the offer. I'm flattered that you thought I could do the job. But as tempting as it is, my future plan is to play professional football, and I need to be ready for that."

"No problem. You're right. You need to stay on track for your career. I admire that in a person."

I was being truthful about my future goals, but I was also relieved at his response. Even though I refused the offer, we remained friends and continued our early-morning breakfasts.

■ ■ ■

Six weeks after starting at the club, I received a phone call from a University of Miami alum who knew some coaches and scouts for the Montreal Alouettes of the Canadian Football League. I didn't know this man or how he got my number, but what he had to say got my attention.

"I know that you want to play in the NFL, but you still have two years before they can even look at you. I've heard that you're keeping yourself in top shape, but that's not the same as actually getting out there on the field. I've been talking with the Alouettes about you. They know what happened at Miami, but that doesn't matter to them. They are very interested in bringing you in."

I had played only five games at Miami, and yet a professional team was interested?

"I'd love to hear what they have in mind."

The emissary did his job. The Alouettes mailed me a contract without ever laying eyes on me in person. They offered me a two-year deal: $30,000 the first year and $36,000 the second year, plus a signing bonus of a couple of grand.

Was this really the best thing to do? I wondered. On the one hand, the experience in the CFL would probably prepare me well for the NFL. But maybe it would be better to finish out my college career first, if there was any chance of doing that. Before I made my final decision, I decided to make a phone call.

I called the coach who had recruited me to Miami, telling him that I had received a contract offer from the Alouettes.

"Could you find out if there is any chance I could come back and finish at Miami?" I asked him.

"I'll get back to you," he said.

I didn't have to wait long for the answer—I was most definitely *not* welcome. I had slammed the door in Miami, and they had dead-bolted it for good measure. And to add insult to injury, he let me know that Coach Saban said I wasn't ready for the pros. In his opinion, I didn't have enough seasoning to even be considered.

After talking with my family about the unexpected offer, I conferred with my "other" family. My job at the club was lucrative moneywise, but it wasn't getting me closer to my dream of being a professional athlete.

"Playing in the CFL seems like a good opportunity," I said between bites of steak and eggs. "I know it's not the NFL, but . . ."

"Personally, I don't enjoy the cold weather in Montreal," my Mob friend said with a smile. "But, hey! If you want to play pro football, then go for it."

That's all I needed to hear. His vote of confidence helped me make up my mind.

Before we left the diner, he said, "And if it doesn't work out, come back to Florida. There will always be a job for you here with us."

I appreciated all of their support and knew that I would miss our early-morning banter when I left for training camp in a couple of months.

■ ■ ■

One night in March I was busy working the door at the club when suddenly I did a double take. "Peggy?" She and her best friend were standing in front of me. She had said she might be coming down to Florida for spring break, but it was still a surprise to see her.

We hugged each other, but I could tell by the look on her friend's face that she did not support any type of reunion between us. Thankfully, she went inside while Peggy stayed outside to talk for a few minutes. I was still on the clock, so I told Peggy to go ahead and enjoy herself. Throughout the night, she'd come out and spend some time with me before returning inside.

Even though it was wonderful to see her again, I played it cool.

For the rest of her stay in Florida, I spent as much time with Peggy as possible. Toward the end of the week, I remember talking about our relationship as we strolled hand in hand on the beach. We both realized that we were meant to be together. We decided to get married when Peggy finished school. Nothing could have made me happier.

The contract was in the Alouettes' hands, and it was time to start packing. But it wasn't only my belongings I was thinking of. I had to pack on some serious muscle before I arrived at camp.

5
READY FOR SOME FOOTBALL

My body weight had dropped twenty-five pounds since leaving Miami—I was now about 235. Even though I was heading to the gym daily, I didn't have the luxury of continuous workouts combined with the nonstop feasting that I had enjoyed at the Miami athletes' training table. And the hot weather made it even harder to keep weight on.

I had always had a fast metabolism and was often kidded by family and friends about how much food I could put away. In my senior year of high school, my voracious appetite earned me the title of the class's "biggest eater," along with my female counterpart, a petite figure skater. We were featured together in a yearbook photograph that showed us lying in mounds of ice cream sandwiches and bags of potato chips. It was pretty common for me to swing by McDonald's between lunch and dinner and grab a Big Mac, a Filet-O-Fish sandwich, a Quarter Pounder with cheese, a large order of French fries, an apple pie, and a milk shake for a "snack." Whenever I went out for pizza with my friends, I would order my own large deep-dish pan pizza with all the toppings and a pitcher of Coca-Cola—just for me.

Now, I had only a couple of months before I had to report to the Alouettes camp. I needed to gain weight in a hurry. At the time, most pro offensive linemen carried between 265 and 285 pounds, unlike today's players, who are well over 300.

For the first time in my life, I considered steroids. Everybody knew who to ask at the local gym. It wasn't an easy decision, though. I had taken personal pride in the fact that I had never touched a steroid before and had managed to break records at Miami without them. But in this instance, with time so short, I thought I might need help. When he sold me the bottle of little blue pills called Dianabol, he assured me it would work.

"Take five pills a day for eight weeks. Eat all the food you can, especially protein, and it will help you put on a few pounds."

He was right. I put on about twenty pounds and arrived in Montreal weighing a respectable 255.

Since I came to the team without anyone actually seeing me in person, I went through the standard evaluations that included everything from my bench-press strength to my speed. My forty-yard dash time, 4.6 seconds, got the same reaction as it had when I was in third grade. The coaches were looking at their stopwatches, and then looking at me. They called the head coach over and asked me to run it again. Still the same time. Everyone was shaking their heads. For most linemen at the time, running forty yards in under five seconds was unusual. The test results, coupled with my bodybuilder-type physique, caught their attention.

That didn't mean a spot on the team was mine. The CFL allowed only fifteen Americans per team—fewer spots than I had originally thought. Somehow they forgot to mention that little detail before I signed the contract. I was going to be competing against veteran US players who had either been on the team's roster already or who were coming from the NFL to claim spots. Not only was I the only rookie player at my position in camp, I was a rookie with limited football experience—a total of five college games. It didn't help that the other seven or eight offensive linemen I saw (all of whom were impressive) were also American. Vying for those two coveted spots was going to be a monumental task, especially with two incumbents in the running.

One returning standout was four-time CFL all-star Dan Yochum. He and future Montreal all-star Doug Payton were both Americans. I started doing the math. The Alouettes would probably keep only two American offensive linemen. Most of the roster spots reserved for Americans were for the speedy skill positions. My back was to the wall. My NCAA eligibility had gone out the window the minute I signed the Alouettes' contract and dropped it in the mail. If they cut me, I wasn't sure what my next plan would be.

■ ■ ■

Offensive line coach Jim Erkenbeck turned out to be perfect for me. With his distinctive gravelly voice, he was a retired Marine who had survived both the Korean War and cancer. Erkenbeck took an immediate liking to me. He wanted me—a long shot—to make the team.

The Alouettes threw me into positions all over special teams—including kickoff coverage and punt coverage. Both units relied on speed and toughness; I wanted to make every play count.

That was especially true in my last preseason game. My job was to be the wedge buster—decimating the three players running in tandem in front of the ball carrier—so my teammates could make the tackle. It's not for the faint of heart; in a matter of seconds, you experience one of the most violent collisions in the game of football. I ran full throttle for thirty to forty yards downfield and hit one of the players in the wedge with such force that I pushed him backward five yards into the ball carrier and took them both down.

Watching the film later with the whole team, the defensive coordinator replayed the clip of that play about five times, marveling each time. "I've never seen this before," he said, laughing. "It's not what we coached, but it was highly effective."

I was young and plenty raw on my football skills, but Coach Erkenbeck saw nothing but potential in me. Still, when I learned that I had made the team as a third offensive lineman, I was totally amazed. All of twenty years old when I got the news, I think I was the youngest American ever to play for Montreal.

Not only did the coach take me under his wing, but so did the Alouettes' all-pro defensive end Junior Ah You. Since I had had such an abbreviated college career, pass blocking was relatively new to me. During practice Junior would tell me what I was doing right and what I was doing wrong, and he even worked with me after practice. It was a fast learning curve, but extremely valuable. Both men helped me tremendously.

I played the first game of the regular season, and then was "hidden" on the injured reserve list. That strategy worked in Montreal's and my favor when Dan Yochum was injured in the play-offs. I was activated to play in the CFL's Super Bowl, the Grey Cup game. At left offensive tackle, I was facing the top defensive lineman in the entire CFL, Dave Fennell. A perennial all-everything for the Edmonton Eskimos, Fennell (nicknamed "Dr. Death") looked incredible on film.

Playing in the Grey Cup in my rookie season? The whole scenario was surreal. On game day, I was fired up, but I was also just hoping to survive. I had a major case of the butterflies. I wasn't sure how I would match up against a player called Dr. Death. I would soon find out if all that extra practice with Junior had paid off.

Early in the game on a running play, I drove Fennell downfield and pancaked him into the turf. From that point on, I more than held my own against Dr. Death. I heard that he had been playing with a bad ankle or knee, but I was still excited that I had been able to contain him the entire game. Unfortunately, the Eskimos, led by future NFL Hall of Famer Warren Moon at quarterback, won 17–9. (I would learn later that Coach Saban had seen the televised game at a sports banquet. For me, it was sweet vengeance to prove him wrong about my readiness to play pro football.)

It was great to end the season on such an exhilarating note, especially leading into a much-anticipated event—my wedding.

■ ■ ■

The setting couldn't have been more perfect when Peggy and I were married on December 15, 1979, at the Penn State University Eisenhower Chapel. Even the weather cooperated, with sunny skies and moderate temperatures. The chapel is intimate and beautiful, ideal for the fifty to seventy-five family members and friends who celebrated with us. Because it happened to be during semester exams, very few of my college friends were able to attend, but they all sent their best wishes.

Peggy and I honeymooned in Hawaii for five weeks, staying in a gorgeous town house along the North Shore of Oahu, with a scenic ocean view. Junior Ah You helped me find an incredible deal since he and his family lived in Hawaii and were involved in the tourism industry.

We swam, played a little tennis, spent time at the Polynesian Cultural Center, and took in as much of the natural beauty of the island as possible. Junior's family made us feel welcome, and we'd often get together for pig roasts and barbecues. There was one unfortunate incident: one day as I charged into the ocean, doing my best Tarzan impersonation, my wedding ring flew off into the water. I grabbed snorkeling gear and hunted for two hours but never found it.

As tempting as it was to stay longer in paradise, we did have to get back Stateside to prepare for my second season with the Alouettes.

I consulted with athletes and other people who were knowledge-able about using steroids. Again, I didn't take the decision lightly. I was concerned about possible long-term side effects. After a lot of discussion, I began an eight-week cycle of both Dianabol and Deca Durabolin (Deca), an injectable steroid, because I was told the two worked well together. Peggy wasn't keen on me taking steroids. I assured her that I was taking them for only eight weeks for off-season strength and size gain.

At training camp in May, I immediately noticed someone was missing.

"Where's Dan?"

Dan Yochum was holding out while he negotiated new contract terms. When he and the team couldn't reach an agreement before the final roster, he was gone.

Our team had another good season and I played well, but we lost in the conference finals.

Peggy wanted to work before we had kids and utilize her degree in speech-language pathology and audiology. She found a position at an elementary school in Syracuse, New York, for the winter of 1980–81, filling in for a woman on maternity leave.

When Peggy was at school, I'd head off to the gym for two to three hours. My job was to eat and train, then eat and train some more. I approached both very seriously. I was a ravenous carnivore, wolfing down all kinds of protein—hamburgers, steak, fish, and chicken—usually with a big baked potato and salad on the side.

Once again, I turned to my reliables—Dianabol and Deca—for my off-season training, this time for a twelve-week cycle. It was all part of my relentless quest to become bigger, stronger, and faster.

■ ■ ■

The winter flew by, and I reported to training camp in early May 1981 for my third season in Montreal while Peggy finished out the school year. Peggy had enjoyed the experience, but she wanted to explore other career possibilities during the next off-season.

I was the starting left tackle for the Alouettes, and after a few games I began to be bothered by a "stinger," a nagging neck injury. I sat out for a couple of plays here and there, but I didn't think it was anything serious.

The team's doctors and trainers had a different opinion. They wanted to give me a game or two off so my neck would heal. Coach Erkenbeck called me into his office and explained what was going to happen.

"We love having you, Lar," he said. "We just want you to rest your injury for a week or two. So we're going to release you on waivers so we can fill a roster spot. It's just the way we do things sometimes. Then we'll re-sign you, and you'll be back in action."

I immediately sensed an unexpected opportunity. As I calmly nodded at everything Coach Erkenbeck was saying, my mind was racing at warp speed. *If temporarily I'm not under contract, then technically I would be a free agent until I re-sign.*

When I left the coach's office, I immediately called an attorney back in Buffalo to clarify what my options were. It was just as I thought: I was under no obligation to re-sign with the Alouettes if I decided not to. It was the chance I had dreamed of—to play in the NFL.

I didn't attend the Alouettes' practice the next day. When someone asked Coach Erkenbeck where I was, he summed it up well: "Larry took the money and ran."

■ ■ ■

Peg and I moved to Buffalo so I could prepare for my move to the NFL. I began working out with Don Reinhoudt, a world champion powerlifter and the 1979 winner of the World's Strongest Man competition. We had met when I was in high school, and I considered him a mentor. I enjoyed pumping iron with him in his garage as I waited for the calls from the pros.

The Green Bay Packers were the first team to fly me in for a workout in late January 1982. I didn't know what to expect. I was weighed, measured, and tested on various skills such as vertical jump, standing broad jump, shuttle run, and the forty-yard dash. I got the "Are you kidding me?" look from the coaches when I finished. In nearly everything, I tested off the charts.

The Packers immediately called me the next morning and offered me a free-agent contract, a two-year deal that paid me roughly $55,000 the first year and $65,000 the second, with an additional $10,000 signing bonus. "If you do well in camp," they said, "you have a good chance of being our starting left guard." I was thrilled.

Everything was falling into place. Peggy was very supportive of my decision to join the team.

■ ■ ■

I was back in Green Bay for my first NFL minicamp in May and quickly created quite a buzz. I had met head coach Bart Starr in January, but on a day-to-day basis I was working with two position coaches—Ernie McMillan and assistant offensive line coach Bill Meyers, an ex-Marine. Everyone was high on me.

Unfortunately, in the first few days of training camp in July, I injured my left hip flexor and groin muscle, which sidelined me for most of the preseason. Every time I felt ready and tried to play, I would reinjure myself. I had gone from a feeling of elation to one of discouragement. With my performance suffering, I could tell the coaching staff was disappointed. The team eventually placed me on the injured reserve list during the 1982 season.

I put my time on injured reserve to good use, spending hours lifting weights for my upper body while my injuries healed. When Coach Meyers would see me in the weight room, he'd make a sarcastic comment, such as, "Well, I sure wish you played football as seriously as you work out." His intuition was right, of course—I did enjoy working out more than practicing football—but I wasn't going to tell him. Still, I saw the handwriting on the wall: I felt that as long as he was my position coach, I was probably not going to play very much at Green Bay.

In 1983 the upstart United States Football League (USFL) arrived on the sports scene, about to begin training camps. The Tampa Bay Bandits, who owned my USFL rights based on where I played collegiate ball, came knocking at my door. Once again, the timing seemed serendipitous. Tampa was a whole lot warmer than Green Bay (which was too cold even for a Buffalo guy like me), and I would avoid the possibility of being benched for most of the season. Before the final cuts at the Packers' training camp, I decided to ask Bart Starr for my release.

I told Coach Starr that I appreciated the opportunity the Packers had given me, but I didn't think things were working out the way everyone planned. He thought about it, talked to his coaches, and granted my request. I was grateful. Within hours, the Buffalo Bills called, wanting to pick me up. It would have been fun to play for the team I had grown up watching, but I was already heading to Tampa with my CFL films.

Once the staff went over the films, they signed me on the spot. I took a little pay cut, but that didn't matter because I was back in Florida and playing Bandit Ball for head coach Steve Spurrier. It was time to finally settle down. Peggy and I bought our first house, one complete with three bedrooms, two and a half baths, a beautiful stone fireplace, and a screened-in backyard swimming pool.

■ ■ ■

Coach Spurrier was known as an offensive genius. He wasn't hard-nosed himself, but his intense offensive line coach, Marty Galbraith, made up for it. It was Bill Meyers all over again, the type of coach I always clashed with.

One day Coach Galbraith called me into his office and chastised me for not eating with the other offensive linemen in the cafeteria. I was so surprised I didn't know how to respond. I hadn't been snubbing my teammates, I was simply sitting with other friends on the team. Besides, it wasn't a rule that all the offensive linemen had to sit together for *every* meal.

"What does that have to do with anything?" I asked him.

"It's important," he snapped back. "It boosts camaraderie and makes the unit more effective."

It was obvious that this was a personal issue between the coach and me, and I felt he was just using this incident as a reason to go at me. Of course, I completely disagreed with him. That had been the story of my football career—I always thought I knew better than my coaches. Fortunately for me, I probably had the best training camp of any offensive lineman. My football skills were progressing nicely, and the rest of the coaching staff loved my athletic ability. At the end of camp, Coach Galbraith didn't pull any punches: he told me that if it had been solely up to him, I would have been released. Yet if he had pushed for my release, I think it would have been apparent that he was putting personal issues before the good of the team.

"You have immense talent," he said. "At Wake Forest, I coached the current starting left guard for Green Bay, and you're better than he is. It makes me wonder why you're not still there."

His comments didn't change my attitude. I thought Coach Galbraith was being a complete jerk. In my mind, I was Tampa's starting left guard who was too good to cut and too good not to start.

But obviously not too good to trade. Four games into the '84 season, I was part of a seven-player deal that sent me to the Memphis Showboats and Coach Pepper Rodgers. The only consolation was that I was far away from Coach Galbraith.

■ ■ ■

Peg had started an administrative job with a Tampa insurance company, so she stayed in Florida while I finished the season in Memphis. I didn't have a lot of playing time for the Showboats because they had their lineup set before I arrived.

When I reported back to Memphis in the spring of 1985, I had a great training camp and earned a starting spot at left tackle. Coach Pepper Rodgers was unlike any coach I had ever had. He treated his players well, and his players played well in return. It wasn't unusual for him to surprise us during practice. After we'd been on the field about forty-five minutes, he'd blow his whistle and bring us all together.

"Gentlemen, it's really hot out here," he would say in his Georgia drawl. "How 'bout we just take the rest of the day off? We got some barbecue and some cold beer over there for you."

His enthusiasm on the sidelines and colorful reactions endeared him to players and fans alike. He always seemed to be having a great time, and I enjoyed playing for him.

Halfway through the season, I tore some cartilage in my rib cage and was sidelined. The Showboats didn't waste any time in replacing me with a high-priced former NFL All-Pro offensive lineman named Luis Sharpe. I was eventually released and finished the season with the Jacksonville Bulls.

It was great to be back in Florida. I didn't know it at the time, but my football career was about to be replaced by something much bigger.

6
LEX LUGER
IS BORN

My grandfather, Stanley Pfohl, loved professional wrestling.

When I was a kid, running around with my cousins at my grand-parents' house in Buffalo on a Saturday night, we'd dart past Grandpa Pfohl sitting in his favorite chair, his eyes riveted to the weekly matchups on the black-and-white television. Sometimes I'd pause momentarily to see what was so captivating, but it didn't grab my attention, so I'd dash off to play.

Now, as I drove to the office of Championship Wrestling from Florida (CWF) in Tampa to see about making some extra money with an off-season job, I wondered if maybe Grandpa's passion really had subtly influenced me, without me knowing it. If he had been alive, I would have asked him a lot of questions.

The first few times I stopped by the office unannounced, the doors were locked. On my fourth visit, a man opened the door suddenly, took a look at me in my T-shirt and shorts, and invited me inside.

I introduced myself. "I'm Larry Pfohl. I'm a pro football player, but I'm looking for some off-season work. I've been seeing and hearing a lot about WrestleMania, but I don't know much about the pro wrestling industry or how you get into it. Is there someone I could talk to about a possible career option?"

"No one's available right now," the man named Danny said. "If you really want to train with someone, I suggest you get in touch with Hiro Matsuda. Here's his number." He handed me a card and shook my hand. I called Matsuda, and we arranged to meet.

The timing was perfect. I had no inkling that professional wrestling was about to change dramatically, with the sport's emphasis turning more toward stars with sculpted physiques. My combination of height and impressive muscularity were just what the promoters had in mind to wow the fans. And now I was about to meet one of the top trainers in the business. The first WrestleMania, the pay-per-view event of the World Wrestling Federation (WWF), had premiered in March. It was seen primarily on closed-circuit TV, with PPV limited to a few parts of the country. The main tag-team event featured Hulk Hogan and Mr. T versus Roddy Piper and "Mr. Wonderful," Paul Orndorff. Hiro Matsuda had trained two of the headliners—Hogan and Orndorff.

Matsuda owned a garment factory in Tampa, and we met in his office there. When I entered the room, he stood up and extended a hand. His grip was strong. He was smaller than I was, but large for a Japanese man at six feet one, 215 pounds. His perfect tan set off his jet-black hair and bright smile; his teeth were such a brilliant white that I swear a person could read by them. Matsuda gestured for me to take a seat. He asked me about my background and a couple of questions about football. And that was it.

"So, do you have a wrestling school?" I asked politely, still trying to figure him out. I knew he was a former pro wrestler. I'd later learn he was an expert in the martial arts and that his training was legendary and fierce; it was rumored that he would snap the bones of students if he thought they weren't taking the training seriously.

"No. I don't have a school. But I do train wrestlers."

I didn't hesitate. "I'd like you to consider training me. I'll certainly compensate you for your time."

Matsuda waved me off, dismissing the mention of money. "I'll let you know."

A few days later, he called, telling me to report to the garment factory in my workout gear.

■ ■ ■

I had always prided myself on my disciplined approach to workouts. But as I would soon find out, Matsuda's method for training was in a class all its own. Before I was allowed to even imagine being in a ring, before a single wrestling move was demonstrated, I had to master Matsuda's legendary regimen and pass the final exam he had created. It was his way of weeding out those who weren't truly dedicated. To him, it was a matter of honor and respect for the sport. Matsuda was protective of his profession and only wanted the best of the best to represent what he loved. Even in someone as raw as I was, he saw something: star potential. I had no clue what it would take to get there or what Matsuda had in store for me. But it was about to be revealed: the unremarkable garment factory by day became my personal torture chamber by night.

From the very first day, Matsuda was intense and precise, like a machine. That appealed to my own work ethic. Our one-on-one sessions always began with a five-mile run in the late afternoon or early evening, when the South Florida heat and humidity were so stifling you could hardly breathe. That was all part of the plan. I was twenty-seven and Matsuda had another twenty years on me, but he did everything he asked me to do. When we got back to the factory, drenched in sweat, there was no cooldown. Actually, there was no air-conditioning, no wrestling pads, no carpet—nothing but the bare concrete floor where the clothes racks had been pushed aside to form an area approximating the size of a wrestling ring. The lighting was dim, cast from a single lightbulb hanging above us and a faint glow from Matsuda's office. It was eerily quiet. The real work was about to begin.

"Ten sets of thirty push-ups." After I did thirty, Matsuda would nudge me out of the way and do thirty; we'd alternate until we reached three hundred. Matsuda counted, but he only counted the ones done correctly—your chest had to touch the floor. The goal was ten minutes or less, two push-ups per second. I really felt it the first two weeks; I could barely lift my arms. But my body quickly adapted.

The five-mile run and the push-ups constituted the pre-training warm-up. There were many guys who never made it past the warm-up stage, or it would take them nearly a year to do so.

The push-ups were followed by one of Matsuda's favorites: hindu squats. Hindu squats work all the muscles in your legs—quads, hamstrings, and calves—as well as your hips, lower back, and lungs. When you maintain correct form and combine the movements with deep breathing, this exercise builds overall body strength and gives you incredibly strong legs with explosive power. The great Indian wrestler Gama used hindu squats to develop tree trunk–size thighs that gave him overwhelming dominance over his opponents. Matsuda liked hindu squats so much that he required a thousand of them on the final exam, with another five hundred hindu jump squats to raise the cardio level and help with coordination. I was thankful that I had been incorporating squats into my own power-lifting routines for years and had strong legs. Still, I was relieved that Matsuda started off with only a hundred or so of each, gradually adding more each time.

It was a grueling two hours. At the end of each session, Matsuda would run and grab a mop to clean up the puddles of sweat on the floor that had poured off of us.

Day after day, Matsuda pushed me. His drive fed mine. *I can do this. I want this.* I was enough of a student of physiology and my own body that I knew that the amount of training I was doing would be a little easier if I dropped ten to fifteen pounds. So I held off doing my now usual off-season twelve-week cycle of testosterone and Deca. I was always being evaluated as to whether I had what it took to make it into the ring. That was never a given for anyone Matsuda mentored; for most students, it was a struggle to achieve the goals he set—and that was before actually learning the fundamentals of wrestling. Within two months, I had passed Matsuda's notorious final exam and officially decided to give up football.

■ ■ ■

Wrestling 101 took place in an old, beat-up television studio in Tampa where CWF's governing body, the National Wrestling Alliance, taped the CWF matches for local broadcasts. The on-site arena, called the Sportatorium, held about a hundred people, fans who sweated out the action with the wrestlers during a match. It wasn't a big improvement over the garment factory. The studio had no air-conditioning, and with its corrugated tin roof, it got crazy hot in the steamy Florida summers. It was like an Easy-Bake Oven; I'm sure there were times when the temperature hit 130 degrees inside.

Once again, Matsuda's training was methodical and meticulous, executed step-by-step and practiced for hours. He wanted every person he trained to have sound fundamentals, and he was a stickler for doing them correctly. Because fans were paying good money to be there, Matsuda wanted his wrestlers to give the crowd their money's worth and make the action as believable as possible. Nothing could look sloppy; it had to be rock solid.

Step 1: Getting in and out of the ring. Yes, this is a learned skill, and some wrestlers never got the hang of it, looking less than graceful.

Step 2: Hitting the ropes. The sides of my body took a beating from this seemingly simple move. I was black-and-blue from my lats to my thighs from hundreds of hits and bounces.

Step 3: Hitting the ropes, jumping up, and landing on your back. This is an exercise to simulate a body slam. You had to jump high, or Matsuda would make you repeat it. There was a little give when you hit the mat, but you definitely felt it.

Step 4: Attacking the turnbuckle. This metal device attaches the ropes to the ring posts and keeps the ropes at their proper tension. The goal is to make the whole ring shake by hitting the turnbuckle with your back and using the momentum to propel yourself forward. Matsuda's goal in all of our training was to make everything look convincing and believable to the fans.

Step 5: Body slamming. Matsuda's philosophy was that you had to learn to take bumps before you could dole any out—the bumps were repeated again and again until you were absolutely fearless. Because he taught the correct way to land on your back—in such a way that every part of your body hit the mat simultaneously— the move looked clean and crisp, while providing maximum protection from injury.

Not to say that a week's worth of body slamming wasn't brutal. It was. As a football player, I was used to being rammed into and roughed up. But to be honest, this constant battering made me extremely sore. As I'd slip into bed next to Peggy each night, my body was completely exhausted, and every muscle was still throbbing. I wasn't about to ice down or do anything to ease the pain. In my mind, that would have been tantamount to admitting weakness. Instead, I simply got up a little earlier the next morning and headed to the gym to work the soreness out. That usually worked pretty effectively.

Finally, Matsuda thought I was ready; I had completed his training faster than any other person had before me. Now it was time for wrestling fans to get their first peek at me, just a teaser to start a buzz.

Since wrestling doesn't have an off-season, my body was going to be on display year-round. So after consulting with various athletes, bodybuilders, and experts whose opinions I valued, I decided that I would now do a twelve-week cycle of testosterone and Deca. Twelve weeks on, twelve weeks off, twelve weeks on, twelve weeks off—like clockwork.

■ ■ ■

Right before the doors opened for the Wednesday morning CWF taping, Matsuda ushered me into the booking office where the conversation among the powers that be had already started.

"Is he going to be a babyface or a heel?"

The "he" was me.

"Heel." Matsuda hadn't explained wrestling terminology to me at all, but "heel" certainly didn't sound like a good guy. (It turns out that my instincts were correct.)

"Should we give him a name or not?"

Most wrestlers' handles are determined by the guys in charge, but because I had fast-tracked through Matsuda's program, no one had even thought about names yet. Except me. *I don't want to get stuck with a stupid name.* I knew it wasn't my place to offer suggestions, but I had done my research and thought if the opportunity came up, I'd throw my pick into the ring.

Everyone was talking around me as if I wasn't in the room. Matsuda, Wahoo McDaniel, and Blackjack Mulligan, among others, were tossing out a few names. None of them seemed to click with the bookers. Still, I was following Matsuda's advice to sit quietly, watch, listen, and learn. But time was getting short; it was only minutes before the scheduled taping.

I raised my hand and broke my silence. "I have a suggestion for a name." They looked at me as if an alien had just landed in their midst.

"All right, kid, let's hear it."

"Lex Luger."

One of my favorite television shows at the time was *Magnum, P.I.* with Tom Selleck. I had looked up *magnum* in the encyclopedia, which led me to research guns. TV's Magnum carried a semi-automatic pistol; I thought, in honor of my German heritage, a Luger would be apropos. It's easy to guess where *Lex* came from—an homage to my favorite superhero, Superman, who battled his villainous archenemy, Lex Luthor.

I had practiced saying it dozens of times: Lex Luger. The bookers looked at each other and shrugged their shoulders. "Well, that's not bad." They decided to go with it.

"So, kid, where are you from?"

"Buffalo."

Once again, I suddenly became invisible to them as the conversation grew more animated in the room.

"We can't use Buffalo."

"Yeah, too small of a market. And who down here even knows where Buffalo is?"

"Let's say he's from Detroit or Chicago."

"Chicago it is."

Sorry, Buffalo. I didn't really disown you. It was just part of my story line. But for the rest of my career I always got booed in my old hometown.

The fans were filing in. It was time for announcer Gordon Solie to interview "Ravishing" Rick Rude and his manager, Percival Pringle, on camera. I was ushered in behind Rude, standing shirtless in the background. I don't remember if anyone mentioned me at all or if the words *Lex Luger* appeared on-screen. They told me not to open my mouth.

To further fuel the fans' anticipation of my wrestling debut,

Matsuda had created a video of me working out in the ring at the Sportatorium—doing sit-ups, hindu squats, and, for dramatic effect, push-ups with a guy on my back. The end of the video was quite refreshing—we went out the side door of the studio, and Matsuda doused me with a bucket of cold water.

■ ■ ■

I had the fundamentals, I had a name, I had a debut date, so now I just had to do some last-minute shopping for my costume. My colors were black and white, my favorite color combination to this day: black tights, white boots, and a white tank top. I was on a budget, so I stopped at an outlet mall and purchased the cheapest tank tops I could find, grabbing dozens of them. I'm sure the clerk was more than a little curious.

It was close to Halloween 1985, and I was slated for an under-card match with veteran Cocoa Samoa at Daytona Beach's brand-new Ocean Center. The arena seated over 7,000 people; ironically, it would be the very first time I'd ever been to a professional wrestling match in my life. I had never been a spectator, and now I was going to be under the lights.

Matsuda made an unexpected but generous offer: he would be my ringside manager for the night. Actually, it was more than generous—Matsuda never went to matches. The fact that he was going to be there, in my corner, was astounding. It was a huge confidence booster for me. *Besides*, I thought, *if I get lost out there, he could help me, either outside or inside the ring.*

I won't lie; I had butterflies. But I also had an enormous amount of confidence and was focused on making Matsuda proud. As I walked out of the locker room and made my way to the ring, the crowd noise was starting to rise. Everything was a new experience for me. I had no idea what to expect. And from the looks on the fans' faces when they saw me, neither did they.

They gawked and pointed, they whispered to each other, and they screamed at me. I saw a lot of mouths dropping open. When I got in the ring and tore my precut tank top off, the roar reverberated off the walls.

As I slowly turned and looked at the crowd, I noticed two young women sitting in the front row. "Oh my gosh!" one screamed. "Now *that's* a man!" Her eyes bulged out like a cartoon character's, so much so I was almost afraid they'd fall out. When her girlfriend let out a piercing scream, the guy between them held his ears and laughed uproariously.

There was a lot on the line for me. I didn't want to mess anything up in front of Matsuda or embarrass myself or disappoint the fans. Interestingly enough, the locker room had emptied out when I left to make my entrance. The other wrestlers on the card were backstage, lining the curtain, eager to watch the match. None of them had ever seen me work before. They wanted to see what I had and how the crowd reacted to me. I could only imagine what they were thinking. *Can this guy even put one foot in front of the other? Does he have any ring skills? Will his performance be halfway decent?*

The ten-minute match flew by and was pretty much a blur to me, although I thought things went reasonably well. I certainly was glad for Cocoa Samoa leading me through the match.

After my debut, Matsuda and I stayed a little longer at the Ocean Center to watch a few more matches before heading home. I would collect my paycheck for a hundred bucks later. My immediate gratification had come when my match ended: Matsuda was smiling.

Before we got on the highway to drive back to Tampa, Matsuda asked me to stop at a convenience store. He was gone for a few minutes, then returned with two six-packs for him and a Gatorade for me. *Beer?* I'm sure the expression on my face was priceless. I didn't know that Matsuda even drank! *Besides, he's Japanese. Don't they drink saki?* Matsuda was in a festive mood. For the rest of the journey, he went over the good things I'd done, pointed out what I needed to work on, and discussed other matches on the card. He talked about what life as a wrestler was like from his own experience and cautioned me about maintaining a fire wall between my family and my profession. He had done extremely well in achieving that, a rarity in the wrestling world. Essentially, he was explaining how to succeed in the business and was preparing me for a career. "Your talent will prevail," he told me. He had never talked as much as he did on that trip. I was grateful for the advice.

■ ■ ■

I was getting more television exposure after my debut in Daytona. The great thing about pro wrestling is that it is so fan driven; they might not be writing the scripts, but they definitely determine who the stars are going to be. And it seemed that I was one of their favorites.

On November 19, 1985, just weeks after my debut, a decision was made that would ignite my career: I would face Wahoo McDaniel for the prestigious NWA Southern Heavyweight Championship. I'm sure that Matsuda emphasized to the promoters that they needed to roll with me fast. He knew that fans craved seeing something out of the ordinary in the ring, someone that they didn't see every day on the streets. My cut physique fit that description. But it was still highly unusual to have a relatively unknown wrestler prepped for a championship so quickly.

McDaniel was a former NFL star who had become a legend on the professional wrestling circuit. Wearing his authentic Native American headdress (he was Choctaw-Chickasaw), Wahoo had already been wrestling for over twenty years. In addition to his storied career in the ring, he also served as the booker for Championship Wrestling from Florida—he developed and approved all the story lines we wrestlers were asked to play out. Wahoo was always friendly to me, but because he was busy with administrative duties, he didn't have time to offer me any technical advice.

Wrestlers usually had little if any say in the story line, although we sometimes talked in advance in the locker room about how things were supposed to play out in the ring. Sometimes we'd rehearse the moves in advance, but usually it was just a matter of communicating to one another in the ring, working together to make the match as realistic as possible.

I'm not sure that Wahoo was particularly keen on the idea of wrestling me at first, especially since I was so green.

"What am I supposed to do?" he asked Matsuda.

"C'mon, you can have a good match," Matsuda challenged the veteran. "You don't think you can lead him through it convincingly?"

I guess no wrestler can walk away from a challenge. Everything went as planned. When I took the Southern Heavyweight Championship belt from Wahoo McDaniel, things began to change rapidly. But that wasn't the only change in my life.

■ ■ ■

In the spring of 1985, Peggy had announced she was pregnant, so we were eagerly anticipating our first baby at the end of January. As we watched the televised New Year's Eve celebration and countdown from Times Square, we toasted each other and our coming baby with sparkling apple juice and snacks of shrimp cocktails and pizza.

At 12:30 a.m., Peggy disappeared into the bathroom. When she had been in there for a while, I called out, "You okay?"

At first, there was no answer. Then she said, "I think my water just broke."

"What does that mean?"

"I think we need to go to the hospital."

Our firstborn wasn't due until January 24. We weren't ready. We hadn't packed a bag for Peggy yet. It was on our to-do list for New

Year's Day morning. The doctor had told us all along that there was no hurry; we could wait until three weeks before the baby's due date.

So much for that plan.

I took a deep breath, calmed myself down, checked on Peggy, and tossed a few things into a bag for her. I was more excitable than she was, but if I appeared nervous, Peggy would be nervous. It was raining and dreary; we arrived at Tampa General Hospital around 2 a.m. It wasn't an easy delivery, but Peggy insisted on doing it without an epidural. I stayed by her side and tried to remember everything we had learned in the childbirth classes.

The first time the doctor left the room, I said to the nurse, "Isn't he supposed to be here?" He'd come back, and then he'd leave again. I wasn't too happy with his comings and goings; I wanted him to stay put. But then I'd focus on Peggy, who was incredibly brave and strong through the whole process. Finally, at one o'clock in the afternoon, Brian announced his arrival with a healthy cry.

It was the greatest sound I had ever heard in my life. Brian was long and gangly with big hands and big feet, obviously taking after me. When the nurse placed my son in my arms, I was relieved and excited. For the next three days, I was on such a joyful high that I didn't sleep a wink and spent as much time as I could with Peggy and Brian. Family and friends stayed with her when I left to go to a match, but I hurried back as quickly as possible. Like my dad had done for my mom and us kids, I wanted to provide well for my family.

When Peggy and Brian came home from the hospital, we established a routine: I'd take care of Brian when I got back from a late-night match so Peggy could grab some sleep. After a few weeks, it was second nature for me to come home, warm a bottle of milk in the microwave, test a drop on the back of my wrist to make sure it wasn't too hot, then get comfortable in the rocking chair with Brian. As he lay quietly in my arms, his eyes never left mine. For a half hour or so, we'd rock, and I would describe the night's match to him until he fell asleep. Those precious moments with my son are some of my most treasured memories.

■ ■ ■

Over the next year I would see a lot of Florida—at least the inside of wrestling venues—since I was working pretty much every night. Wednesday was always the longest day because we'd do our TV taping for Saturday's show, film all of our interviews for the specific individual markets, then hop in the car to drive to Miami or another city for a match, and finally return to Tampa. I usually didn't arrive home until about 4 a.m., but at least I was home every night. I'd spend time with Brian, catch a few hours of sleep, then head to Rick Poston's gym for an early workout.

Rick was an accomplished professional bodybuilder and former Mr. America who had been helping me transition my workouts from being football-focused to wrestling-oriented. He knew how to build muscle mass. Not surprisingly, when I approached him about steroids, he told me how bodybuilders used them, as did elite athletes in other sports. Most of his gym's clientele were serious athletes, so Rick was a knowledgeable resource. In the couple of years that I had been using steroids, I had approached them scientifically, researching what was available and monitoring my body's reaction carefully. I had heeded the advice regarding the importance of clearance: eight weeks on, eight weeks off; twelve weeks on, twelve weeks off. It was critical to give my body time to rebound. Matsuda probably knew I was taking something; but I never discussed my usage with him, and he never asked.

As my popularity began to rise, my salary increased to a main-event level, about $1,000 to $1,500 per week. I was beginning to be noticed outside of Florida, too, by various NWA territory rivals, including Jim Crockett Promotions of Charlotte, North Carolina. When one of

Crockett's stars, NWA world champion "Nature Boy" Ric Flair, came to Tampa for a series of regional matches, I was one of several wrestlers over several nights scheduled in the ring. It was a boost to any region when a world champion came to town because a star billing filled the house. Flair was flamboyant, smooth-talkin', and the star of NWA pro wrestling—and I was facing him for the first time.

We were slated for a "broadway," a time-limit draw; in this case, an hour-long match. I learned what the plan was just minutes before I left the locker room. *An hour-long match?* The longest I had been in the ring prior to this had been ten or eleven minutes—max. I was nervous and a little worried.

In the midst of the match, Flair told me to use a sunset flip on him. *A sunset flip?* Even though it was one of the most basic moves in the sport, I didn't have a clue what he was talking about. There was a momentary look of disbelief on his face, then he got to work. For the next hour, Flair carried me. But here's the thing about Ric Flair: no matter what an opponent's skill level, he can make the guy look like a million bucks—he was that proficient. I was relieved when it was over and extremely appreciative to Ric for what he had done.

Afterward, when I was in the locker room, I overheard him talking to my promoters. "You've got an incredible talent here, and the crowd's really reacting to him. You need to bring him along and start teaching him more moves. This guy is going to be big!"

Obviously, my popularity with the fans wasn't based on an endless repertoire of skills. They were eating up "the look." I had relied on what Matsuda kept emphasizing as my "gift." "Always show your body, and don't try to do what the other wrestlers do. Stick to the basics and show your body. That's what people are going to pay to see."

But I had to ask him about what I had overheard Flair say. Was it important for me to learn a lot of new moves in the ring?

Matsuda wasn't worried about me. "Some of these things you need to know, some you don't. You'll learn over time."

In 1986 I was named Rookie of the Year by *Pro Wrestling Illustrated*, gracing the cover of its *Inside Wrestling* magazine—one of countless covers I would be featured on with various wrestling publications over the years.

■ ■ ■

My education in wrestling had only begun. For instance, I didn't even know the difference between the WWF (World Wrestling Federation) and the NWA (National Wrestling Alliance), other than the first one was headed up by Vince McMahon and the other by Jim Crockett and other promoters throughout the country, including the one I worked for. I certainly didn't realize how deep the rivalry was between those top two organizations. I didn't have time to get into the history or the business of things. Wrestling kept me busy enough. I knew who Ric Flair was and that he was the marquee member of the NWA's Four Horsemen, but I had no idea who the other Horsemen were or what they looked like.

I wrestled Flair a few more times after that memorable broadway. Flair continued to be high on my potential and obviously was talking me up to Crockett. Toward the end of the year, Crockett called.

"We'd like to bring you up to Atlanta and put you on our Saturday night TV show."

That Saturday night show, *World Championship Wrestling* (later known as *WCW Saturday Night*), was filmed at the old Techwood Studios on 14th Street and was aired on Ted Turner's superstation WTBS. It would be my first time wrestling outside of Florida and would mean national TV exposure to wrestling fans. Crockett wasn't making me any offers or promises. He just wanted to see me in person.

I was certainly excited, and even more so when some of my fellow wrestlers said what a big deal it was to be given the opportunity.

Matsuda seemed guardedly happy for me. He never actually said

so, but I knew he was probably concerned about Crockett's intentions—and the real possibility that if I went, I'd be gone for good.

For the next few weeks, I'd fly up to Atlanta on Saturday mornings for the show, then return to Florida for an evening card and
wrestle throughout the rest of the week. I was still employed by
Championship Wrestling from Florida. But after my premiere in
Atlanta, the story line of the Four Horsemen was about to undergo
a plot twist.

7
RIDING WITH
THE FOUR HORSEMEN

As soon as Jim Crockett and the bookers saw me in person for the first time, they began creating a new Four Horsemen story line that would include me.

The Horsemen were Ric Flair, Arn and Ole Anderson, and Tully Blanchard, with manager J. J. Dillon. The group had formed in June 1986, pulling together a team of heels with incredible individual talent. Flair was reigning world heavyweight champion, the Andersons (not related in real life) from the Minnesota Wrecking Crew had been world tag-team champions, and Blanchard had the NWA world television champion title.

The new story line centered around Ole Anderson taking time off to watch his son compete in high school wrestling. His devotion to his real family rather than his Horsemen family infuriated the others. Ric, Arn, and Tully didn't like Ole's "snot-nosed kid" who

WRESTLING WITH THE DEVIL

was interfering with business, and Ole's loyalty to the group came into question.

Against this developing story, I was just wrestling whoever Crockett threw into the ring with me. The goal was to give me the most TV exposure and build up my fan base. Ric already knew what I could do, but J. J., Arn, and Tully had to see for themselves. They began scouting my matches with keen interest.

It wasn't long before I became part of the story, brought into the fold as an "associate," with Ric making my on-screen introduction: "He can wrestle. He's got style and profile. He's got class." Weeks later, Ole's days as a Horseman came to an end with a group beat-down, before we threw him into a broom closet.

I was no longer an associate: I was one of the Four Horsemen. Everything about me was about to get a makeover.

When you become a part of wrestling royalty, you need to look and act the part. Jim Crockett Promotions's main booker and wrestler in his own right, "The American Dream" Dusty Rhodes, began thinking of exactly what my "something extra" would be.

I was backstage with Dusty, the other Horsemen, and J. J. before the Saturday taping.

"What can Lex do to get the crowd on their feet?"

"How about adding a signature move?" someone suggested.

"I'm not convinced that he needs one," Dusty said. "He should simply stick with power moves, lots of body slams and clotheslines, things that will showcase his body."

Suddenly, a technician threw out an idea. "How about the backbreaker? It would be a great way to show off his body, especially his abs and legs, as well as his overall strength."

I was open to anything, so the technician gave me a quick runthrough on how the move was supposed to be done. We practiced backstage, minutes before heading out to the ring. When the time was right during a match, I would power slam my opponent, then flex my upper body to signal to the crowd what would become my signature move—"the Torture Rack." While my opponent was still dazed, I'd come up behind him, grab him, and lift him onto my shoulders until he submitted.

"That's it!" Dusty slapped me on the back as I headed to the locker room after the match. "We all loved it! That's your finish!" And it had all come together five minutes before showtime.

That's wrestling in a nutshell—you ad-lib as you go, and go with spontaneity when you can. In my wrestling career, some of the best things happened on the spur of the moment.

I had a signature move. Now I needed a descriptor. Before one of my first interviews as an official member of the Horsemen, Dusty was giving me a pep talk. "You need to show a little more swag in front of the cameras, the kind of bravado that makes the Horsemen the most loved and hated group of all," he said. "Exude confidence. Let everybody know that you have the brains, the brawn, and the professional football pedigree. You're the total package."

The Total Package. Everyone loved the way it sounded, and we quickly passed it on to the announcers to include in the introduction. (I later took an attorney's advice and trademarked both "Lex Luger" and "The Total Package" to retain creative control.)

Things were falling into place almost overnight. Two men had gotten me here: Hiro Matsuda, who gave me the opportunity, and Ric Flair, who was in the process of making me a star. Ric taught me how to read what the crowd wanted and what to do in response. He was a master technician and tactician, explaining the finer points of specific moves, such as the pile driver, which was a fan favorite.

"When you get a guy up there, hold it," Ric said. "Hold it for five to ten seconds. Let everybody see your strength, see that six-pack you've got."

Not only was Ric a great teacher outside the ring, he would lead me through the moves and talk me through an entire match in the ring. It was almost like having a night off, because I didn't have to think about what the next move would be. With his experience, Ric knew what the payoff was: if I looked good, he looked good, and the fans would eat it up.

I also needed a new costume. The tank top was history; the promoters didn't want me looking like some Hulk Hogan wannabe. It didn't fit the classier style and persona of the Horsemen. I was expected to dress the part, in and out of the ring. Ric wore handmade robes that were true works of art—you could be blinded by the sparkle alone under the lights. He put me in touch with Olivia Walker, the woman who designed them. For my inaugural entrance as a Horseman, she created a long, black silk robe with "Total Package" in silver on the back. I never thought I'd wear anything with rhinestones in my life, but the end result was spectacular, with a price tag to match—$5,000 out of my pocket.

My family and I moved to Charlotte, where we leased a house.

If I thought my wrestling schedule in Florida was hectic, I hit the ground running—er, flying—now. I was wrestling one night in Charleston, West Virginia, then flying across the country with the Horsemen the day after for an evening match in Inglewood, California, heading to San Francisco, then back to Cincinnati and Pittsburgh, all within six days. Thank goodness for frequent-flier programs, because we were on planes a lot. All of this was leading up to The Great American Bash on July 18, 1987, at the American Legion Memorial Stadium in Charlotte, North Carolina, where I was defending the NWA US heavyweight championship against Nikita Koloff in a steel-cage match.

There was some crowd-inciting choreography that night. Koloff came into the ring wearing a neck brace, but I ripped it off midway through the match. J. J. Dillon "assisted" me by throwing in a steel chair, and I hit Koloff in the back. I used the torture rack to knock out the defending champion and celebrated my new title of US heavyweight champion in the ring with Tully and Arn.

With my victory added to Ric's world championship title and Arn and Tully's world tag-team title, all the gold and glory belonged to the Horsemen. We had everything, and everybody either loved us or loved hating us.

Whenever we arrived at a venue, there was a palpable sense of excitement in the air. As Ric liked to boast, "We were a bunch of limousine-ridin', jet-flyin', wheelin'-dealin' sons of guns," a carefully made image with roles that we played masterfully.

We genuinely liked each other. In the locker room, with no cameras running, there was a lot of verbal jousting and good-natured ribbing. Arn's sharp tongue and quick wit kept us laughing, and he had a knack for coming up with memorable nicknames for the others—and now, for me.

The first one came out of his mouth at a steel-cage tag-team match in Los Angeles that pitted me, Ric, Tully, and Arn against the Road Warriors, Sting, and Dusty Rhodes. The cage hadn't been set up properly; instead of it being outside the ring, it was inside the ring! There was nowhere to go—we were standing so close to the action that it looked really lame and completely unrealistic to us, let alone the fans. As Arn and I stood a few feet away from Ric and watched him take a beating, I said, "What should we do?"

"Shuddup, Eggplant!" Arn shouted at me.

Eggplant?

"You just stand there and look good, and let me do the thinking."

Arn also liked to kid me about the size of my teeth. "Willlburrr . . . ," he'd draw out the name in a perfect imitation of Mister Ed, the talking horse on the sixties' TV sitcom. Eggplant or Wilbur—I laughed at and answered to both. And dished it right back.

Our camaraderie was great, which helps when you're spending so much time together. Their motto was "work hard, play hard." Even though my focus remained on working out and wrestling, I definitely didn't want to let the rest of the Horsemen down. Especially on the weekends, we would knock back a few. And sometimes more than just a few.

Within a few months, I was livin' large, just like the other Horsemen. Now it was time to get paid like one.

■ ■ ■

I had never signed any formal contract with Jim Crockett Promotions (JCP). My paycheck was two or three thousand a week, comparable with most wrestlers' main-event earnings at that time.

Wrestlers had always worked under unilateral contracts: agreements with no specific money stipulated. It was a long-standing practice for promoters to pay guys according to where they appeared on the card. The more popular and high profile you were, the later your name appeared on the card and the more money you made. The WWF was no different. Vince McMahon used unilateral contracts too, paying his performers at his discretion based on card placement.

But things suddenly changed for me after I returned from a wrestling event in Las Vegas. There, I had randomly bumped into Vince McMahon at the gym. I had never met him before, but I certainly knew who he was. We exchanged pleasantries and talked for five minutes about our families; wrestling was never mentioned. But that's not the message that got back to Jim Crockett. Little did I know how much gossip dominated professional wrestling at the time and what a flurry my conversation with Crockett's rival would cause. I overheard some whispers that Jim Crockett was seriously concerned because I'd been seen with Vince. As soon as I got back to Charlotte, I was called to Jim's office.

"Look, we got you on TV, and you're one of the Four Horsemen. We need to get you under contract."

I was happy to sign a contract; I had signed contracts when I was playing professional football. He handed me a standard contract, but as I skimmed through the pages, I didn't see any mention of money. I was concerned about being locked into a contract without that important detail in writing.

So I spoke up.

"I don't see any kind of compensation mentioned in here."

"We don't do that."

"So let me get this straight. I sign with you, you own my rights, I can't wrestle anywhere else—but there's no money stipulated? No minimum guarantee? Nothing?"

He leaned forward and looked at me while I continued. "I don't mean to be ungrateful, Mr. Crockett. You've given me a great opportunity, but this just doesn't seem right. I need to be sure that I can provide for my family."

"What do you think you should be making?"

"I'd like to be able to make what Ric Flair or Dusty Rhodes makes. If I'm able to reach their popularity level and I'm producing, I'd expect you to pay me as much as you pay them."

"Well, give me a figure that you consider to be fair," he replied.

"I'll have to think about that. I'd like to confer with my attorney."

"Okay," Jim said. "Let your attorney look over the contract and bring it back with a figure."

The truth was I didn't have an attorney; I was bluffing. But I kept my composure, thanked him, and agreed to meet with him again the following week.

A week later I returned with the contract, requesting a guaranteed $350,000 minimum per year, a huge amount of money at the time. Would my bluff pay off?

If we had been playing poker, it would have been a very short game. It took Jim Crockett only a matter of seconds to mull it over.

"Okay, we'll do it. A three-year deal paying you a minimum of $350,000 annually. Give us a week to get everything drawn up."

Because I was feeling empowered, I said one more thing.

"Can we get first-class airfare, too?" I asked.

"All of you?"

At that time, Ric was the only Horseman who flew first class; Arn, Tully, J. J., and I always sat in coach. I thought it sent the wrong message to fans and sullied the image of the Horsemen as athletes accustomed to only the finer things in life.

I tapped my inner lawyer and presented my case.

"The Four Horsemen have to maintain the image of opulence that's been crafted. Fans are everywhere, including the airport. When a plane lands, how would it look for us to be some of the last passengers to get off instead of the first? I think it's bad PR."

"I see your point. We'll take care of that, too. Anything else?" he said sarcastically.

"No, that'll do it."

With everything agreed, I left the building feeling so pumped I could barely keep from shouting and jumping in the air. But I didn't want to spoil the surprise for Peggy, who was waiting in the car. I calmly got into our white BMW.

"So what happened?"

"It's done," I said quietly.

"How much?"

"You're not going to believe this. They went for it. Three years, $350,000 per year. And first-class airfare to boot."

The smile on Peggy's face was priceless.

"Guess what, Peg?" I said, grinning back at her. "We're millionaires! We're rich!" Jubilant, I began slamming my hands against the inside of the car so hard it started to rock, while Peggy bounced up and down in her seat. If anyone had walked by at that moment, they would have thought we were both crazy.

As we pulled out of the parking lot, I leaned toward her and said, "Hey, Peg, do you think I should have asked for more?"

The quest for more was just beginning.

■ ■ ■

It was back to business, but things would never be the same. The figures in my contract had somehow been released. I was learning that nothing in wrestling is a secret. I was upset for guys like Arn and Tully (among others), who had been in the business longer than me and were making far less money. They wouldn't be jumping for joy when they learned about my salary, but no one said anything to my face. They did routinely joke about it, though.

"I can't believe Eggplant here is making more money than all of us," Arn would laugh. "What was Crockett thinking?"

What I quickly deduced was that being a Horseman was a 24-7, 365-day gig with no breaks. It was like being a member of a high-profile rock band. Rabid fans were everywhere—in the airports, at our hotels, in the parking lots, at the arenas. They'd even follow us to local restaurants after we were done with our matches. I don't know how they were able to track our whereabouts, but whatever system they used worked extremely well. Included among those fans were women who were known in the industry as "ring rats"—wrestling groupies—many of whom were available for whatever you might be interested in.

In less than a year as a Horseman, I had become a household name and a proven commodity. Toward the end of 1987, the story line was set to be rewritten once again. The powers that be decided it was time for me—the reigning US heavyweight champion—to part ways with the Horsemen and wrestle as a babyface (good guy) for the world title against Ric Flair the following summer.

The scriptwriters began setting the stage for unrest between me and the other Horsemen. At Starrcade '87 in Chicago on November 26, I was in a steel-cage match against "The American Dream"

Dusty Rhodes. At the end of the match, J. J.'s role was to toss a metal chair into the ring for me to use on Dusty. But the "plan" backfired, and it cost me the title.

On camera after the match, I pretended to be upset with J. J. about what had happened. In subsequent interviews, the rest of the Horsemen began talking down to me because I had lost my title. It wouldn't be long before all of this drama would come to a colorful climax.

8
THINGS ARE A-CHANGIN'

As the words from the Neil Sedaka song go, "Breaking up is hard to do." While that may be true in the world of romance, in my case—with the Horsemen—breaking up was fun.

At the Bunkhouse Stampede Championship on January 24, 1988, at the Nassau Coliseum on Long Island, I thwarted J. J.'s game plan for him to win the stampede championship. The scriptwriters were building a story line where I would challenge Ric Flair for the world heavyweight championship, something I couldn't do as one of the Horsemen. But, of course, the final split had to be dramatic.

It happened a few weeks later, with cameras rolling. Ric, Arn, Tully, and J. J. had arrived at the predetermined location ahead of me, waiting in the shadows of the parking lot for me to arrive.

Since the beginning of my wrestling career, I had never been asked to "get color," i.e., intentionally be cut to bleed, during any of my matches. This occasion called for it, and I was game. But I didn't want to mess things up on my first attempt.

We decided J. J. would have a razor blade taped on his finger to "get color" on me. Before I got out of my limo, I was instructed to wash down four aspirin with a couple shots of Jack Daniels. That combo would thin my blood so I would bleed better. In the ring a wrestler is sweating and his heart rate is up, so bleeding is no problem at all. But in this scenario, I needed some help. We wanted to be sure there would be lots of red on my white tuxedo.

As I got out of my limo, the others "jumped" me and started roughing me up. When one of them banged my skull against the trunk of the car, I busted my head wide open. That wasn't the plan, but it certainly worked well. J. J. swiped the razor blade across my forehead for good measure. The moment the cameras cut away, I wrapped my head in a towel. By the time we got to the luxury hotel in Coconut Grove, my tuxedo and the makeshift turban were soaked in blood. I could feel the blood squishing in my shoes as we walked through the lobby. The looks on the faces of both the staff and the hotel guests in the lobby were priceless. Hours later, up in my room, I was still bleeding from the gash. I phoned J. J. and asked him to come to my room and look at my wound.

"Should we go to the hospital?" I asked J. J.

"Nah, you'll be fine. It's in your hairline. It'll be okay."

Relieved, I joked with J. J. "By the way, your razor cut was pretty crooked."

He just smiled and said, "Yeah, I guess we didn't need it after all."

I went from heel to babyface instantly and was now on the hunt for the Horsemen, especially Ric Flair. However, so was someone else: Steve "Sting" Borden was regularly matched up with Ric. He had become an immediate fan favorite when he had debuted at WCW's Starrcade '87. I kept my eye on him from a distance, checking out his matches and reading what others were saying about him.

In many respects, we were in direct competition with each other—in the ring and behind the scenes. The two of us were featured on the summer 1988 cover of *Wrestling* magazine. We were constantly being evaluated by a combination of our TV ratings, buy rates and pay-per-views, merchandise sales, and fan reactions. As much as I wanted to find fault with him, I couldn't. Well, except for one thing.

One night I was backstage with Ric. He and I were watching Sting's pre-match interview on the TV monitor in the locker room. The fans were eating it up. When Sting was done, I commented, "That interview made no sense at all. It was dumb."

"I know, Lex," Ric said. "He's just *got* it."

What Sting had was the "it" factor—an inexplicable combination of energy, natural talent, and charisma that elicits excitement every time that wrestler is in front of the crowd. The promoters recognize it, and the fans embrace it.

In the spring of 1988, Sting and I were in the locker room after we had both wrestled when Sting approached me. I had just finished the last match of the night and was bent over in my chair, untying my boots.

"Hey, man, I've been checking out your matches and notice you always stay in great shape," Sting said. "How do you eat and train to maintain that on the road?"

"Stolis [Russian vodka] and peanut M&M's," I responded sarcastically, not even bothering to look at him.

I did glance up when I heard him turn and walk away. He was shaking his head in disbelief.

Over the next few months, we started running into each other everywhere—at house shows, in the same hotels, at breakfast in the morning, at the gym working out. Finally, we started having breakfast and going to the gym together. As we got to know each other and became traveling partners, we found out how much we had in common. It was the beginning of a profoundly deep friendship.

■ ■ ■

The feud between Ric and me generated big money for Crockett Promotions, and they were hoping it would be enough to keep the company solvent. But by the end of 1988, Crockett was still struggling financially and was behind on paying me my guarantee. I felt like I needed to look at my options.

After talking with my attorney, I contacted Vince McMahon and told him that we felt Jim Crockett was in breach of contract. Vince invited me to his house for a secret meeting. I flew to Greenwich, Connecticut, and we spent the entire morning together. It was a great meeting. Vince made us tuna fish sandwiches for lunch, one of my favorites. His parting words were, "I'd love to have you. Let's allow this to play out a little more, not only for my company's sake, but for your benefit too." I think we both knew that sometime in the future we would enjoy doing business with each other.

Shortly after my secret meeting with Vince, Ted Turner bought out the wrestling assets of Jim Crockett Promotions and created World Championship Wrestling (WCW). The terms of my contract remained intact even with the change in ownership, and that suited me just fine. I didn't anticipate any financial problems from a savvy, world-renowned businessman like Ted Turner. For the moment, life was good, and I moved my family to Atlanta.

In 1989, Sting and I became business partners and opened our first gym together in Atlanta: Main Event Fitness. It made perfect sense, since both of us knew our way around gyms. Our eventual goal was to franchise Main Event Fitness. It was one part of my master plan to create a fitness and nutrition empire someday.

■ ■ ■

Even more exciting than a new business or a championship title was the news that Peggy was expecting again. The baby was due in late

October 1990. I was extremely busy traveling, but I resolved to move heaven and earth to be there when our second child was born. We didn't know if the baby was a boy or a girl. However, Peggy and I had agreed that if the baby were a girl, she would be our last child. That meant it would be especially important for me not to miss this event.

Peggy experienced some scary moments during this pregnancy, more so than when she was carrying Brian. Several times it seemed like the baby was going to come prematurely. It happened in early August and again in early September, but the doctor was able to give Peggy some medication to stop the contractions. The doctor explained that it was important to keep delivery from happening too soon in order for the baby to grow and to minimize any potential health issues. Each time Peggy called, I was ready to hightail it to the closest local airport and hire a private plane to get me home if necessary. Fortunately, those were all false alarms.

Finally, toward the end of September, the doctor thought we could schedule a date to induce labor safely. The baby would still be premature, but not dangerously so.

On the morning of September 24, 1990, Peggy and I checked into Northside Hospital in Atlanta. They induced labor, and we had our beautiful baby daughter, Lauren. As I held my precious baby girl in my arms, I felt sheer joy and relief at the same time. She was perfectly healthy and had made our family complete.

■ ■ ■

In the meantime, my career and Sting's were both on the rise. One unforgettable match we wrestled in together was SuperBrawl I in St. Petersburg, Florida, on May 19, 1991. It was a rare face-versus-face match with the two of us wrestling the Steiner Brothers, the reigning world tag-team champions. Pulling off those kinds of matches was always difficult because when good guys are squared off against one another, the crowd doesn't know who to root for.

Wrestling insiders predicted it would be a real stinker. What often happens in this type of matchup is that one of the babyfaces has to cheat to win, which most fans don't buy into.

But for this event, Sting had a brilliant strategy. He recommended that we all go all out, performing our signature moves in succession on one another. Fans would be kept guessing because there would be no clear good guy or bad guy. We fed off the crowd and let their reactions direct the action, wowing them with all our best stuff—suplexes, running clotheslines, pile drivers, and just about everything else. It was pure genius. The crowd loved it.

We were all very happy with the outcome. Even Ric came up and congratulated us afterward, saying, "Man, guys, I hate having to follow that match."

Ric wasn't the only person to pay us a compliment. *Pro Wrestling Illustrated* named it the 1991 Match of the Year.

■ ■ ■

The WCW world heavyweight championship title held by Ric Flair still eluded me. However, the baton was about to be passed. I was scheduled for a steel-cage match at the Great American Bash in Baltimore on July 14 for the final blowoff between Ric and me. This title match had been years in the making.

Unbeknownst to us, Ric was embroiled in a contentious contract battle with WCW officials. Talks continued up to the day of the match, with the WCW brass still holding out hope that they'd be able to keep Flair in their stable. Unfortunately, Ric walked. We had to go to a contingency plan. Barry Windham was stepping in as the number two contender to face me for the now-vacant world heavyweight title.

"If you wrestle Barry and cheat to win, you will be our heel champion," booker Dusty Rhodes explained. "We've flown in former world champion Harley Race to be your manager. I'll have Harley slide the belt under the cage at the end of the match, and I want you to use Harley's finish—the pile driver—on Barry on top of the belt."

"And one more thing. At the end of the match, don't hold the belt up. Ric took the belt with him when he left, and we didn't have time to make a new one." They had slapped a makeshift belt together and wanted to be sure the ringside photographers didn't take a picture of me holding up a phony belt. I found it all pretty humorous; after years of such a buildup, at the last moment we were all scrambling around like the Keystone Cops. Despite all the last-minute problems, the match went just as planned, and I left with the title.

Ric's move to the WWF was a huge loss to the WCW. There was a lot of unrest and uncertainty in the WCW front office, which began to really concern me. Personnel cutbacks were being made, and I knew I didn't want to be known as their marquee austerity champion. I felt it was time to move on, and I had to find a way to make that happen. So my first call was to Vince McMahon.

Vince had launched a new organization—the World Bodybuilding Federation (WBF)—which was going to showcase a group of professional bodybuilders through a weekly television show, *WBF BodyStars*, leading up to a pay-per-view championship in June 1992. On the phone, I threw out an idea to Vince. "What do you think about signing me to a one-year WBF bodybuilding contract if I can get out of the last year of my wrestling contract with the WCW?"

I was already planning to sit down with my current employer to ask for a year off. "I'll tell them that I won't be wrestling anywhere for a year but may possibly explore other opportunities. If they agree, I can be a bodybuilder for you and then segue into wrestling the following year."

Vince was intrigued by my proposal and said he'd get back to me.

My next meeting was with the WCW front office, where I made a confession. "I've been going hard for six years. I'm burned out and need a year off to rest and be with my family."

That was certainly true, and since I suspected the company was looking for more places to save money, I thought it could be a win-win situation. So I wasn't surprised when they responded, "We can't pay you if you aren't wrestling for us."

"That's okay. I might be looking into some other opportunities over the next year, but wrestling will definitely not be one of them."

I didn't elaborate; I let them think what they wanted. They accepted my offer, and we both agreed to the terms.

Meanwhile, Vince had gotten back to me. He agreed to sign me to a WBF contract, assuring me he would take care of me financially. It was a sweet deal.

I didn't feel as if I were doing anything unethical or anything that might have been considered a breach of the deal I had reached with WCW. I wasn't wrestling for Vince, I was simply showcasing my body.

Things got somewhat nasty, however, a little while later when WCW officials saw me promoting *WBF BodyStars* in a commercial running alongside promotions for the WWF's upcoming WrestleMania. The WCW officials were irate. They sued, claiming I had violated the terms of our buyout. But since I never attended WrestleMania, let alone wrestled on the card, the legal action wasn't viable.

■ ■ ■

I had two big events to go as the WCW world heavyweight champion. The first week in January 1992, I appeared in the Tokyo Dome in Japan to defend my world title. I felt the international exposure was a great opportunity to expand my relationships with promoters and fans around the world.

February 29, 1992, would be my last appearance as the WCW world heavyweight champion. That night, in Milwaukee, I would turn the title over to Sting at SuperBrawl II.

I showed up at the arena just before it was time to make my entrance. I know Sting wasn't happy with me. For one thing, he hated it when I was late to anything. He has always been the ultimate pro and wants to put on a good show for the fans. He had looked for me before the match to discuss our strategy in the ring, but I was nowhere to be found. I was being elusive on purpose—I just wanted the match to be over and done with, and for me to emerge unscathed. We got the job done.

Now I could finally focus on getting ready for Vince's show, which was slated for the summer. I worked hard, getting myself in the best shape of my life, even to my own critical eye.

Two weeks from the airdate, life was about to change again.

■ ■ ■

One evening in June 1992, Peggy was getting ready to put some salmon and asparagus on the grill for dinner.

"I'm just going out for a quick spin on the bike. I'll be back in fifteen minutes," I said to her, grabbing my full motorcycle helmet instead of my stylish half-helmet that I usually wore with sunglasses during daytime rides. I thought my customized turquoise-and-white Harley was beautiful, but I didn't feel Peggy shared my enthusiasm. I had taken her out for a ride right after I had bought the bike. When I tried to make a tight turn in the cul-de-sac, the bike tipped over. We both jumped off in time, but Peggy never got on the bike again.

It was dusk as I started down the two-lane road. I had a route I liked to take from our residential area to the more rural, forested Georgia countryside.

As I approached a long, sharp curve at forty-five or fifty miles an hour, I realized I was going too fast to hold the bike on my side of the road. With the sun disappearing, the curve had snuck up on me. So midway through it, I started moving to the middle of the road, still blind to what was ahead and hoping no one was coming the other way.

But someone was. Coming out of the curve, I saw the car with two teenagers inside. The young driver's expression was wide-eyed in panic, and the girl next to him was screaming. Like me, the driver had drifted to the middle of the road to execute the curve.

I steered more to the left and gassed it, hoping to avoid a head-on collision. In that split second, I also lifted my right leg up so it wouldn't get crushed between the bike and the car. The impact catapulted me into the air—I was soaring like Superman for a few seconds. I was aware that my feet were flying up over my head, and from my years of wrestling I knew what that meant. If I didn't do something fast, I would land on my neck or my head. So I put out my right arm to break my fall.

Amazingly, I didn't hit any trees; I just bounced about 150 feet down the wooded slope, doing twisted cartwheels that made me feel like I was in a clothes dryer. I couldn't keep my legs from splaying. I almost felt like I was being split in two. When I finally stopped, I was lying with my feet pointing up the slope.

My first thought was, *Am I alive?*

Once I had established that, I looked at my left arm, which had been gashed in several places. Since I was only weeks away from appearing on Vince's WBF pay-per-view extravaganza as a guest poser, my only thought was, *Man, these gashes won't look good onstage under the lights.* My next thought was, *Don't lie here. Get back up to the road.* I could move my legs, but I had trouble sitting up.

I felt a strong stinging sensation in my right arm. I was wearing a tank top under a baggy, three-quarter sleeve workout pullover. I pulled up my sleeve, and my right arm looked like it was going to fall off. It was dangling like a wind chime, nearly severed just above the elbow. Below my elbow, bones were sticking out four or five inches. Blood was everywhere. I lay back down and tried wrapping the right sleeve tightly around my elbow to make a tourniquet. I said to myself, "This is bad."

It was getting dark, and I could sense people around me. I could hear them, but I couldn't see them very well with my helmet on. (Recently, I met a couple who had been a few cars behind the driver who hit me. They saw me fly through the air, and the woman—who found me in the woods—told me she stayed by my side praying until the paramedics came.) I'm not sure what happened to the two teenagers in the car.

Once the paramedics arrived, they refused to remove my helmet and strapped me to a backboard, which killed my tailbone. While lying in the ambulance, speeding to North Fulton Hospital in Roswell, Georgia, I thought it had all been a bad dream.

I was stabilized at North Fulton, but the doctors kept me on the backboard because I was too big to lift easily. I distinctly remember a nurse saying, "You'd better be thanking God that you're alive. People involved in motorcycle wrecks like yours are usually DOA."

"What's DOA?"

"Dead on arrival."

I so desperately wanted to see a familiar face. I was busted up, in a lot of pain, and—for the first time in my life—I was filled with true fear. I felt scared and helpless.

Finally, a face appeared that I knew. Sting was hovering over me, and boy, was I happy to see him. He had come as soon as he had gotten home from his match and heard the news from his wife, Sue.

I was so thirsty and dehydrated at that point. I said, "Stinger, I need some water." When the staff wasn't looking, he got a gauze pad, soaked it in water, and squeezed it over my dry, cracked lips. Man, that felt good.

Before Peggy got there, Sting overheard the doctors talking on the other side of my bed in the emergency room.

"He's going to have to lose the arm," one of the doctors said. "There's just too much damage."

I was hearing bits and pieces of the conversation, including a word that caught my attention. When I heard the doctor mention the word *prosthesis*, I was horrified. I immediately envisioned myself wrestling as a "Captain Hook" character.

Sting was infuriated at what he felt was their lack of professionalism; instead of discussing the prognosis with me, they chatted about me as if I weren't even there. But the reality was that I wasn't about to sign any papers giving them permission to amputate my arm. Sting took matters into his own hands and contacted Dr. Jim Andrews, a world-renowned sports medicine and orthopedic surgeon from Birmingham, Alabama. Dr. Andrews was known for treating not only professional wrestlers but also many other professional athletes. While Sting paged Dr. Andrews, Peggy finally arrived.

Not knowing what had happened to me all those hours and fearing the worst, my wife was an emotional wreck. She was upset and angry. I thought, *Here I am, the most scared I have ever been in my life, and she's angry at me?* I was looking to be soothed and consoled. I took her reaction the wrong way. I didn't consider that she had suffered a shock too—believing that she and the kids might have lost me forever. When she began to get light-headed from seeing all of the blood on the floor, they had to assist her out of the room.

Sting heard back from Dr. Andrews immediately. He agreed to do my surgery in Birmingham. That was welcome news. I wanted to leave North Fulton with my arm intact. The North Fulton staff followed Dr. Andrews's instructions to fix the dislocated elbow and finally give me some pain medication.

I was transferred to Birmingham the next day. I had lost so much blood, it was necessary to delay the surgery. Dr. Andrews worked wonders, inserting a titanium plate in my arm. He admitted afterward to me, "When I first saw the damage, I thought, *I can't do anything with this.* But then I put that together and then that together, and I realized, *Maybe I can do something with this.*"

Fortunately, my vision of being "Captain Hook" never materialized. With the surgery a success, Dr. Andrews had no doubt that I'd eventually return to where I had been physically. I did need to give my bones time to heal, which meant I couldn't lift weights for a few months. After that, I would only have a short period of time to get ready for my WWF debut, which was beckoning.

9
JUMPING TO THE WWF

The Total Package was going to be rewrapped. But Vince wanted a unique twist to my character. "Everybody knows you as Lex Luger, 'The Total Package,' but let's get them thinking of you as 'The Narcissist,'" Vince excitedly explained.

In Greek mythology, Narcissus was known for his physical beauty (including his physique!). One day when Narcissus passed a pool of water, he was drawn to his own reflection and became so enamored with it that he wouldn't leave.

A marketing and character-development genius, Vince thought the self-worship angle was an ideal fit for me, especially since I was always striving for the perfect body in real life.

I was training steroid-free for the unveiling and my debut because of the stringent mandatory drug testing that was taking place for all the wrestlers in the WWF. I was pleasantly surprised that I could look as good as I did without steroids, so I didn't take any during my tenure at the WWF.

I was unveiled in a guest appearance at the sixth annual Royal Rumble that was held at Arco Arena in Sacramento, California, on January 24, 1993. I stood alongside my manager, Bobby "The Brain" Heenan, draped in a silver cape before lifting it to show my physique. The idea was to tease WWF fans with a taste of what was to come a few short months later.

Actually, I was still healing from the motorcycle accident and not physically ready to resume wrestling. But Vince wisely figured that this would be a great way to start the buzz and build up the anticipation for my pay-per-view appearance while I continued my rehabilitation.

Two months later, I was ready for my WWF debut. The buildup crescendoed when I entered the arena for the pre-match introduction at WrestleMania IX, held at Caesars Palace in Las Vegas on April 4, 1993. I had done a few house shows prior to that, but this was the event where most of the world's wrestling fans would watch me perform in the WWF for the first time. I walked toward the ring, flaunting my self-indulgent attitude, accompanied by beautiful showgirls who held up large mirrors for me to admire myself. My entrance was much more dramatic than my opponent's— "Mr. Perfect" Curt Hennig.

Curt was renowned as a great worker and one of the very best tacticians and technicians in all of wrestling. I was thrilled that they'd chosen him to work with me at WrestleMania. It was hard for anybody to have a bad match with him because he could bring out the best in anybody, just like Ric Flair.

I wasn't considered a premiere worker. I had always followed Matsuda's advice, "Keep it simple." I was best known for simply flexing my muscles and showing off my sculpted physique, so the pairing seemed like a great idea. The two of us had talked in advance about how we were going to structure the match and were confident that we had everything covered.

As the match began, I was startled when Curt and I locked up and he said, "What are we doing?"

"What do you mean, 'What are we doing?'" I shot back, the panic building in my voice. "Aren't you the one leading this match?"

"I'm drawing a blank! I'm drawing a blank!"

"Oh, no! Now what are we going to do?"

Somehow we managed to get through the match with me leading. As you can imagine, it wasn't exactly one of my best matches or even one of the better ones on the card, so I was glad when it was over.

Over the next few months, my career as The Narcissist was going well. Fans reacted enthusiastically wherever I went. In June, Vince asked me to come to his office at WWF headquarters. I didn't know what was up; it was highly unusual for him to pull a wrestler off the road for a meeting. That's when he surprised me with a new story line: I was now going to be one of the organization's star babyfaces, a coveted position. My days as a heel were over. I would soon be revealed as "The All-American," the WWF's most beloved patriot, introduced at an exhibition aboard the USS *Intrepid*.

■ ■ ■

Located at Pier 86 on the west side of Manhattan, the famed aircraft carrier had been commissioned in World War II for service in the Pacific against the Japanese, provided air support for American troops in Vietnam, and dispatched helicopters to pick up NASA astronauts in the 1960s after they returned from their missions. The warship, now a permanent museum, had patriotism written all over it.

It seemed fitting that the exhibition was scheduled on July 4, 1993, with WWF world heavyweight champion and Japanese wrestler Yokozuna, who challenged anyone to body slam him—all six hundred pounds of him. He claimed it could never be done.

Yokozuna, boasting that nobody had ever lifted him off his feet, began the exhibition with twenty of the biggest, strongest athletes on the planet—NFL players, NBA players, wrestlers, powerlifters, and bodybuilders—all taking turns at trying to slam the mammoth man down, with no success. Yokozuna laughed at their feeble attempts.

"Is this the best America has?" he scoffed, much to the chagrin of the crowd on hand to celebrate the nation's birthday. "Americans are so weak! Isn't there anybody in America who has what it takes?"

While Yokozuna was inciting the crowd, I was climbing aboard a helicopter a few miles away for a hair-raising ride. The pilot was under extreme pressure to land on the ship at the exact moment planned, so once I got in, we were airborne. The door was wide open, and I didn't even have my seat belt buckled before we were speeding on our way. I held on to the seat for dear life. I was convinced I was going to fall out of the helicopter and plummet into the Hudson River below!

As the helicopter began its descent to the ship, fans aboard the *Intrepid* were momentarily stunned, unsure of what it was doing there. Then I popped out in a distinctly all-American look of faded blue jeans, cowboy boots, and a red, white, and blue shirt as the *Made in the USA* theme song blasted through the speakers. I shoved my heel manager, Bobby Heenan, aside and jumped into the ring to defend my country's honor.

Yokozuna was massive, but I always called him "the dancing bear" because he was so incredibly nimble for a man his size. He was undoubtedly the most talented big man in the business. Because of his immense girth, it was difficult to reach and grab Yoko—let alone slam him.

He had to help you, of course, but even then, picking Yoko up required coordination and perfect timing. It was imperative that your

THE EARLY YEARS

At the beach with my dad. Look at those golden curls!

The Pfohls all dressed up: my mom, me (left), my sister, Barb, and my brother, Barry

With sweet Daisy, one of three Saint Bernards I grew up with

Showing some style in my high school senior portrait

READY FOR SOME FOOTBALL

Excited to be a Hurricane at the University of Miami. I was touted as a future NFL player even as a sophomore.

The Pinto with the exploding gas tank. I drove that junk heap all the way up to training camp in Montreal.

With my parents at Christmas after my rookie season with the Alouettes. Dad loved the hat, at least for the photo.

Brian and me in the backyard pool at our first house in Tampa

With trainer Hiro Matsuda, celebrating my first big title—the NWA Southern Heavyweight title I won as a rookie in 1986

LEX LUGER IS BORN

"The Total Package." Dusty Rhodes first used the phrase to describe me in a prematch pep talk.

A clean sweep of gold. In 1987, the Four Horsemen (left to right)—Tully Blanchard, Arn Anderson, Ric Flair, and myself—had all the NWA/WCW championship titles, under J. J. Dillon's management (far back). I was the US heavyweight champion, Tully and Arn were world heavyweight tag team champions, and Ric was the world heavyweight champion.

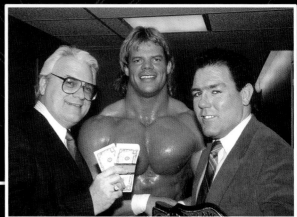

J. J. Dillon (left) flashing the cash to Tully Blanchard and me during Horsemen days

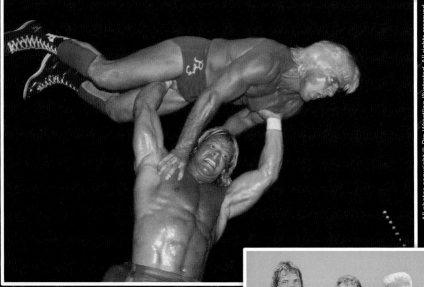

One of my countless matches against Ric Flair

FRIENDS, FOES, AND FAMILY

The first time Sting and I teamed up. We defeated Arn Anderson and Tully Blanchard for the Crockett Cup in 1988, and Magnum TA (center) presented the trophy to us.

Sting and our kids hanging out together about 1991. Sting is holding his firstborn son, Garrett, and my children, Brian and Lauren (lying down), are on the trampoline with another friend.

My beautiful daughter, Lauren, and me celebrating her first birthday

My first world title victory against Barry Windham took place on July 14, 1991, at the Great American Bash in Baltimore.

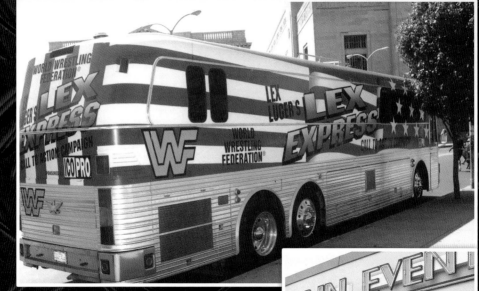

For six weeks, I barnstormed across the country in the Lex Express, making appearances everywhere from local TV shows to shopping malls. It was part of the promotional buildup to SummerSlam '93.

THE QUEST FOR SUCCESS

Sting and I were co-owners of this Main Event Fitness gym, the first one that opened in Atlanta.

Polishing the pecs with some cable crossovers inside the gym, the end of a heavy chest workout

Feuding with two of my greatest challengers: Yokozuna and Hulk Hogan

While recovering from my injury, I went to the Shepherd Center's chapel every day to find comfort, strength, and encouragement for what lay ahead.

A WHOLE NEW LIFE

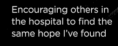

Encouraging others in the hospital to find the same hope I've found

Today, I enjoy meeting and working with up-and-coming wrestlers who love the sport as much as I still do.

feet were set correctly to provide a strong foundation for him to come up on you so that you could turn him. It required really powerful legs, or he'd run completely over you and make you an ink spot on the mat.

Yoko and I had rehearsed everything about a week earlier at the WWF's nearby headquarters in Connecticut. I had been in my running shoes that afternoon; now, I was in cowboy boots. The boots certainly added to my look, but I knew immediately there would be problems. As soon as I slid into the ring, I began to lose my footing.

When we were nose-to-nose, I began to panic. "Yoko, I'm not gonna be able to do it, I'm not gonna be able to do it. I feel like I'm on ice skates in these boots! I've got no footing."

"No problem, brudda," he said calmly. "I got ya. Just do your best to stay on your feet."

As scripted beforehand, he took a swing at me, and I ducked under it before countering with several powerful blows. Yoko rebounded as he was supposed to and tossed me into a turnbuckle.

As he charged me in an attempt to squash me in the turnbuckle, I was supposed to jump out of the way at the last second. When I moved, Yokozuna would hit the turnbuckle and then stagger back out, facing me, so that I could body slam him.

Yokozuna slowed up enough as he bounced off the turnbuckle to avoid running me over before performing an acrobatic turn in midair that gave me the footing I needed. In essence, he sort of body slammed himself.

The crowd went absolutely nuts. On camera, I looked pretty excited, but the truth was that I was more relieved that we had pulled it off.

My professional persona was suddenly as all-American as Mom and apple pie. And just like a politician, I was ready to meet my adoring fans during a barnstorming campaign to build up excitement for my shot at the WWF title against Yokozuna at SummerSlam.

■ ■ ■

I met lots of moms, dads, and kids—fans of all ages—when the Lex Express bus rolled out for the six-week cross-country promotion. After the exhibition in July, Vince had said to me, "If I put the world title on you, I'm not sure if it will be at SummerSlam or at next year's WrestleMania at Madison Square Garden."

I wasn't concerned about whether or not I was going to get the heavyweight title. That was Vince's decision, not mine. As always, I trusted his instincts. I knew that this promotional tour was a way to give a big push for an individual character leading up to a pay-per-view event.

There were three of us riding down the highway together—a driver, a publicist, and me. We pulled out of the WWF headquarters in Stamford, Connecticut, and began the whirlwind trip. At the first stop in Danbury, Connecticut, we met eight thousand fans waiting for my autograph at Meeker's Hardware store, a historical landmark. Four hours later, I had to stop signing and just shake the rest of the fans' hands so we could head to Boston. It was nonstop from 5 a.m. until 9 p.m. in city after city, small and large. The publicist and others had done their jobs well on relatively short notice to give me the most exposure on a variety of media. In the early mornings, I'd be featured on radio talk shows, do local TV talk shows, fit in two autograph signings a day at large stores or other venues, stop at local landmarks for photo ops, make guest appearances on early-evening news shows, do a segment with the weather guys, and if I had any energy left, I'd try to hit a gym and work out, too. I didn't travel with any security; we were on our own. I would catch a nap on the bus when I could, and we would stay at hotels to get some needed sleep before going hard the next day.

Fans showed up in large numbers everywhere we went. I distinctly remember a huge crowd in Denver, Colorado—the line snaked around a Toys"R"Us twice. I don't know how many showed up, but it was extremely hot that day, so bottles of water were handed out to everyone. At Mount Rushmore in South Dakota, the plan was for me to stop for a photo op. As soon as we parked the bus, it was swarmed by fans. I had to use the fire escape hatch to get up on the roof, where I posed with four presidential faces behind me. Vince flew my family in to travel with me on the bus for a few days, which I greatly appreciated.

We put serious miles on the Lex Express—hitting states from the East Coast to the West Coast and back.

On August 30, 1993, at the Palace in Auburn Hills, Michigan, the SummerSlam showdown took place. Yokozuna and I began the match. However, I don't remember much after that. One of his leg drops was slightly off, and his backside landed on top of my head. I was dazed for most of the remainder of the match. With such a massive body hitting me, my head could have been crushed like a coconut. Luckily it wasn't. The truth was, Yoko was a careful technician in the ring. He knew if he ever got sloppy, someone could get seriously hurt. I was glad it wasn't me that night. The match ended with a countout, with Yokozuna unconscious outside the ring. It wasn't the world title win that most of the fans in the building were hoping for.

Vince decided to keep Yoko and me separated until WrestleMania X in March.

■ ■ ■

With the US economy in a slump, the wrestling industry was feeling some of the fallout too. But Vince always had a plan B. Because the WWF was global, we traveled to shows in Canada, Europe, and other parts of the world to give the domestic market a rest. The arenas abroad were always packed, since we rarely traveled overseas. Even though portraying The All-American could be challenging abroad, I was relatively well received wherever we went.

At that time, one of my traveling buddies in the States and abroad was Bret "The Hitman" Hart. I have to be honest—Bret is responsible for one addiction I still have to this day. It started when we landed at O'Hare International Airport in Chicago for a show.

We had gotten our bags into the rental car and were ready to head to our hotel.

"Wait!" Bret said. "I have to run back inside the airport and get some coffee!"

"What? We can get coffee at the hotel."

"No, I have to get it here."

"You mean you're going to go back through security to get some coffee?"

"Yeah. Wait here and I'll be back."

Bret came back with two cups of Starbucks dark roast coffee. I wasn't a coffee drinker before that cup of Starbucks—I had gotten my caffeine from energy drinks—but from that moment, I was hooked. For years, Bret was my coffee buddy whenever we'd travel together. In Europe, one of our first priorities would be to find the closest café. Today, I am always ready with my Starbucks Gold Card.

■ ■ ■

Traveling had its perks and its challenges. It was great to see new places. But at times, it could become grueling. We had to carry so much stuff, we felt like pack mules. I would always carry one bag specifically for my wrestling gear, one bag full of workout clothes, and a third one for street clothes. I did get packing down to a science—I just rotated the clean stuff to the top and moved the clothes I had worn to the bottom of my suitcase in plastic bags, separated by towels.

I was doing more than separating clothes in my suitcase; I was starting to fall into a double life, separating my life on the road from my life at home. I remembered Matsuda's advice about creating a fire wall between my profession and my family. But I used it to rational-ize what I was doing. Everywhere we traveled, women were there. There was a serious unwritten code called "the wrestler's honor." Whatever happened on the road, stayed on the road. It was nobody's business to tell another wrestler's wife or girlfriend about anything that happened, especially when it came to other women. If you broke that code, you were blackballed by your peers.

It happened slowly, but the infidelities began to creep into my life. I would meet an attractive woman at the gym or the tanning salon or a restaurant—or wherever—in the cities on the circuit. So I'd think, *As long as I go home and am a devoted husband and father, I can keep the two separate and distinct.* It was a secret life with no accountability—or so I thought.

I felt that there was enough silence among my peers and enough distance from my family to keep my infidelities from Peggy. Back then, there weren't fans with camera phones who could catch you in an indiscretion and immediately put it on the Internet for all the world—and your family—to see. Still, if I was honest, I knew my actions went against everything I had been taught. I had been raised by my parents never to lie; now I was living a lie.

■ ■ ■

On January 22, 1994, Bret Hart and I were among the thirty wres-tlers assembled at the Providence Civic Center in Rhode Island for the main event on the card: the Royal Rumble match, whose win-ner would face Yokozuna at WrestleMania X. In a royal rumble, it's every man for himself, with a new challenger coming into the ring about every two minutes. There is only one rule: you eliminate your opponent—or opponents—by throwing him over the top rope. His feet must touch the floor outside the ring. The last man standing in the ring wins.

On this night, it was scripted that Bret and I would be the last two men in the ring. In the end, before the finish, Bret was supposed to cross-body me over the top rope and to the floor, where it was hoped we would both land simultaneously. Bret executed this move so well that not even the camera replays could detect who hit the ground first. It was pure luck. WWF president Jack Tunney made the final determination: we were cowinners, which was a great story line.

"That's just our good coffee mojo, Bret," I told him afterward.

Two days later on *Monday Night Raw*, the announcement was made that we both qualified for WrestleMania X—and a shot at the title against Yokozuna.

■ ■ ■

WrestleMania X was slated for March 20, 1994, at Madison Square Garden. Peg and the kids came up from Atlanta and stayed with me at the Plaza Hotel that weekend, in a beautiful suite overlooking Central Park. We had a nice weekend together.

I wrestled Yoko first (determined by a coin flip), and Curt Hennig was our special referee (he was usually a heel). Vince had already told me I wouldn't win the title. Curt did some shenanigans in the ring and disqualified me. That created a feud angle between Curt and me after WrestleMania. I was looking forward to working with Curt, but unfortunately it never came to pass because Curt and the management couldn't come to terms on a contract. Later that night, Bret took the world heavyweight championship title, and I was truly happy for him.

After WrestleMania X, they brought in "The British Bulldog," Davey Boy Smith, who at the time was Bret Hart's brother-in-law. Just like Bret and I had, we hit it off immediately. We began working out and traveling together on the road, enjoying each other's company. We had a lot in common; our kids were even the exact same ages. When we worked in England, we stayed at his parents' house and would drive around in his green Jaguar sedan. It broke the monotony of traveling on the bus and staying at hotels. Eventually, we were scripted as a tag team, known as the Allied Powers. We became a hit with the fans, especially in Europe, where Davey Boy was wildly popular. He was like a British rock star.

In late 1994, no one in the WWF was making big money because of the economic slump. My two-year contract was coming to an end, and it was time for me to renew. I was thinking of ways to make money on top of my wrestling contract, so I asked Vince if I could do some things outside of wrestling with fitness and nutrition. He said he'd think about it and get back to me. In the past, he'd often been burned by wrestlers who would ask to do "extracurricular" things and then never come back.

As negotiations continued, my contract expired in March 1995. I was now working for Vince on a handshake. We were both still optimistic that we would reach an agreement.

By the late summer, an innocent phone conversation between Sting and me would redirect my future.

10
SURPRISE, SURPRISE, SURPRISE

Sting and I had remained the best of friends and business partners, even though we were working for two different companies. We stayed in touch by phone on a regular basis, and when we were both home, our families got together as often as we could.

In August of 1995, we were catching up on the phone when I mentioned that I was technically not under contract with the WWF.

"Wait a minute," Sting stopped me. "What do you mean you're technically not under contract?"

"I haven't been under contract for six months." I explained what Vince and I had been discussing and that I was working on a handshake until we agreed to terms.

I could hear the disbelief in Sting's voice as he clarified for himself what I had just said. "So you are not under any written contract for Vince McMahon, but you're still on his television series doing house shows for him?"

"Yeah."

"So contractually, you're a free agent right now."

"Well, I'm not planning to go anywhere, but yes, technically you're correct."

And then he gave me the scoop. The WCW was planning to go head-to-head against the WWF on Monday night television with a live show called *Nitro*, in the same time slot as WWF's show *Raw*. The WWF had always dominated the television ratings for wrestling, while the WCW remained a distant second.

The new show sounded exciting. "That's pretty cool!" I said.

"Man, have you ever considered coming back here?" Before I could respond, Sting continued, "If you ever have, now might be a good time. If you don't mind, I'll make an inquiry with Eric Bischoff." Bischoff was essentially the Vince McMahon of the WCW.

"Well, I guess it couldn't hurt," I said, not thinking it would amount to anything.

It didn't take long before Sting called me back and said, "Eric's interested in possibly bringing you back. He wants to talk to you about it in person."

Since all of this information about the upcoming program was hush-hush, the three of us arranged a secret meeting at Sting's house. I had met Bischoff before, but this was the first time I had ever sat down with him. He was intrigued with the idea of my return to the WCW, but he made two things clear:

(1) There weren't going to be any big financial guarantees, and (2) the element of surprise was critical.

"Are you saying I can't give Vince any kind of notice?" I asked him.

"That is correct."

"Wow, I'm not sure I'm comfortable with that. Can I think about it?"

"No problem, but I'd like to know as soon as possible if you decide to come with us," he replied.

■ ■ ■

Between that conversation with Bischoff and the final weekend of August, I had received another revised contract from Vince, with many points of contention that we still needed to work out. I was disappointed that we weren't closer to an agreement, but I was still hopeful. I left a message for Vince to call me at his earliest convenience. I carried that revised contract with me wherever I went. Just in case we connected on the phone, I wanted to have it in front of me. He finally called on September 1, 1995, in the early afternoon, catching me before my scheduled Friday match that evening in Moncton, New Brunswick.

It was a cordial conversation, but after I hung up the phone, it suddenly hit me. *We're not any closer on this than we were six months ago.* In my heart of hearts, I believed Vince was trying to come up with something, but I realized it just wasn't going to happen. My options were clear: I would either wrestle for Vince under a standard contract, or I would do something else.

After taking a few hours to think it over, I called Sting. "Can you find out if the WCW offer is still on the table?"

I heard from Eric Bischoff two days later, on September 3. If I agreed to keep everything under wraps, he would fly me to Minneapolis the next morning. *Nitro* was being launched live from the Mall of America that evening. We would work out the contract details later.

This was a crucial decision for me. Vince had been very good to me, and I was very uncomfortable leaving under these circumstances. Although I felt torn, I had to think about my family and what I needed to do to take care of them. I talked to Peggy about it because I valued her opinion. She was supportive and said she would trust my judgment.

At that point, I made the decision. I was in. After my last WWF match teamed up with Shawn Michaels that evening in St. John's, New Brunswick, I was heading back to the WCW.

■ ■ ■

The whole thing was a covert operation. I left on a morning flight, was picked up from the Minneapolis–Saint Paul International Airport by a van, and was driven to an out-of-the-way hotel—far from the other wrestlers' hotel, where the fans usually gathered.

Ordinarily, we were expected to arrive at a venue six to eight hours ahead of time for a televised show. But to make sure the element of surprise wouldn't be spoiled, I was going to be picked up right after the show got underway.

When I arrived at the Mall of America, I had a towel over my head and was immediately escorted to the inner bowels of the mall, well away from the locker room and central concourse area where everything was happening. It wasn't until that moment that I knew how it was all going to go down. "At the very end of the show you'll come out in your street clothes," Eric told me, "and get nose-to-nose with Hulk Hogan."

Everything was going to be live, which was different from what Vince was doing at the time with *Raw*. Initially, *Raw* had been live, but when the costs began to rise, Vince changed the format: he would do one show live, then pretape the following week's show on Tuesday to air the next Monday. But Bischoff believed that doing every show live gave you more flexibility to add any number of surprises.

My entrance was definitely a surprise—to the crowd and to the other wrestlers gathered there.

I walked up to Hogan and said my line: "I'm back at the WCW to wrestle with the big boys."

I was still up in Hogan's face when they signaled for a short commercial break. Knowing we were off the air momentarily, I broke character and smiled at Hogan. It was a big mistake.

"Wipe that grin off your face, or I'll knock it off. You're stealing money from me and my family right now," he said to me through gritted teeth.

I immediately stopped smiling.

After the show I tried to apologize to him, but he brushed me off. I learned a big lesson from him that night: never break character when on camera in front of the fans—even on a commercial break.

The following week, Hogan and I were scheduled to wrestle. Thankfully, we did sit down beforehand, and I sincerely apologized to him for what I had done. He reiterated how important the smallest details are and that staying in character is how we make our living. It was an old-school philosophy of wrestling, something that Matsuda certainly had taught both of us. You'd have to be living under a rock to not know what Hogan had done for our industry. He deserved the utmost respect from everyone, and I wanted to make amends. "I will never let that happen again," I assured him. He accepted my apology, and from that time on, we had a mutual respect and maintained a great working relationship with each other.

My surprise appearance succeeded in creating the kind of buzz we were looking for with the fans. Other than the momentary snafu with Hogan, everyone felt good about my return.

I did hear from some of my friends at the WWF afterward that Vince was extremely surprised and disappointed about the way things happened, especially that I didn't give him any notice.

Unfortunately, he wasn't the first or the last person I would disappoint.

Still, the deed was done. Now it was time for the wars to begin.

11
MONDAY NIGHT WARFARE

The initial ratings for *Nitro* were good, and in the months that followed, our audience continued to grow. We hadn't yet surpassed Vince in the TV ratings, but we were certainly on the upswing. I was back as Lex Luger, The Total Package, feuding with Hulk Hogan and eventually partnering with Sting. Things were going really well, and I felt my career was progressing.

After my debut I signed a pretty standard two-year contract with Bischoff, with the assurance that he would take care of me as things progressed. He proved to be a man of his word. Before the end of my first year, we renegotiated my contract for significantly more money.

Meanwhile, part of reestablishing myself in the WCW was wanting to look my very best. So after talking with some people whose opinions I valued, I decided to go back on my twelve-week cycle of steroids. I felt the benefits outweighed the risks. Although there was testing going on at the WCW, it wasn't nearly as frequent or stringent

WRESTLING WITH THE DEVIL

as what I had experienced in the WWF. There, you never knew when you'd be asked to take off your shirt, drop your pants to your knees, and pee into a cup in front of the tester.

I was told that in the WCW we had more privacy when providing our samples. We could carry in a hidden, false sample with someone else's clean urine, or—worst case scenario—we could slip some Visine into the sample, which nullified the results.

In July 1996, less than a year after *Nitro* went live, the WCW introduced a new story line. Bischoff began bringing in guys one by one from the WWF—starting with Scott Hall, then Kevin Nash—to eventually ally with Hogan (soon to be known as Hollywood Hogan). Hogan would surprisingly turn heel. These "unsanctioned" heel wrestlers were invading and wreaking havoc in the WCW as The Outsiders, taking on Sting, myself, and the other established WCW guys. As they grew in number, they called themselves the New World Order (nWo), and that story line became a sensation. I hadn't seen a group of heels go over this big since the Four Horsemen.

Monday after Monday, at the end of *Nitro*, the nWo would ambush the WCW wrestlers in some way and lay us out in the ring, which riled up the fans. They got angrier and angrier because The Outsiders had incredible heat—that ability to make fans instantly despise you.

And then, being lowered from the rafters, Sting would come to save the day, wielding a baseball bat and scattering The Outsiders from the ring.

Over time, the fans grew so incensed at the nWo guys that they started throwing things into the ring, trying to pelt them with beverages. Soon they began throwing food like nachos and hot dogs and—even nastier—their cups of chewing tobacco spit. The trouble was, most of the garbage wasn't hitting the nWo guys—it was hitting us, the ones lying on the mat!

Immediately after the end of the show's taping, I was often tapped for the non-televised singles "dark match." In this attempt to leave the sellout crowd on a high note instead of a downer, I'd be fighting against one of the nWo wrestlers when the cameras were turned off. I had to move quickly.

One minute I'd be lying in the ring, covered with nacho cheese and other nasty, slimy stuff, and the next minute I'd be coming back down the aisle to my music, ready for the dark match. At first I would try to scramble to change my costume, but it took too long. Eventually, I figured out a quicker solution: I would run to the locker room, jump into the shower in my full wrestling gear, boots and all, and quickly rinse off, before going back out for the dark match.

I'd often tease Sting and say, "Can we switch parts sometimes, so you are in the ring covered in nachos, and I come down from the rafters?" He'd just smile and say, "Somebody has to do that."

I relished my role as the WCW go-to guy. I was doing house shows Thursday, Friday, Saturday, and Sunday, then working the live shows on Monday nights. That's when I got my nickname Cyborg. It was a golden era for the WCW and its wrestlers as the ratings skyrocketed. Beginning mid-1996, *Monday Nitro* owned the TV ratings with a winning streak that would last for eighty-four continuous weeks.

■ ■ ■

After the shows, we celebrated our success. That tradition became more than just knocking back a few beers. For the first time in my life, I started mixing pills with alcohol. When I was on the road, I started doing it on a regular basis. It gave me a bigger, faster buzz. I began to like how it felt and would hold off eating anything in order to prolong the effect. But I still wanted to take care of myself, so eventually I would say, "Let's go get something to eat, guys." I didn't think it was a big deal. It was the "work hard, play hard" philosophy that prevailed in our industry.

I was extremely focused on reestablishing my wrestling career with the WCW. Although womanizing had become a natural habit for me, I decided to put it on the back burner. However, I was still surrounded by lots of beautiful women, and it was a struggle for me to do the right thing.

As time went on, the WCW added more and more women to the payroll: *Nitro* girls, valets, members of the production crew. On Monday nights after the show, we all got together as a group. At that time, as I watched some of the guys go off with the women we saw every day, I thought, *Who would be stupid enough to get involved with someone you work with?* It was an observation that would later come back to haunt me.

■ ■ ■

The WCW kept building up their feud with the nWo, leading to a world heavyweight title championship between Hogan and Sting. We strived to keep the story lines fresh and unpredictable, so the script-writers decided to throw our fans a bone—one that surprised even me.

Hogan and I would wrestle for the championship title on August 4, 1997. And I would win.

Talk about rocking my world! In his entire career, Hogan had never been defeated on national television. And I was the guy chosen to do it. The truth was that Hogan had to approve such a stunning turn of events. He didn't have to do anything he didn't want to do, since he was one of the few guys in the industry who had creative control, allowing him to dictate his own story lines. Hogan had earned that right because of the huge numbers he drew and what he had done for the industry. Such power was pretty much unprecedented in our business; in the history of wrestling, only Andre the Giant had been given such freedom before.

When Eric Bischoff told me that the whole story line was Hogan's idea, I was greatly honored.

Once again, I was privy to a secret that only Bischoff, Hogan, and I shared. The referee didn't learn about it until a few minutes before the match, on his way out to the ring.

At the end of the match, when I got Hogan in the Torture Rack and won the title, the crowd went berserk. It was one of the most exhilarating moments of my career inside the ring.

I lost the title to Hogan in a pay-per-view match the following week at Road Wild in Sturgis, South Dakota, but we definitely accomplished what we set out to do.

And it certainly didn't hurt the *Nitro* ratings either. Fans continued to tune in every week because they were afraid they'd miss something and were anxious to see what was going to happen next.

■ ■ ■

In late 1997, once again Eric Bischoff renegotiated my contract early for even more money. Things were really rolling now. Over the many years I had been on the road and away from home, my family and I had given up a lot. I truly felt that all our hard work and sacrifices were finally paying off. It was time to enjoy the fruits of our labor.

The master plan was going extremely well, and I wanted our lifestyle to reflect that. I used to love watching the television show *Lifestyles of the Rich and Famous*. Now that we had this extra money, I didn't want to hold back.

My family and I moved into a new home on the ninth hole of the Sugarloaf Country Club in the north Atlanta suburbs. It was like something out of *Southern Living* magazine, with all the amenities at our disposal. Our lavish backyard with a full-size swimming pool was absolutely picturesque, with a gorgeous panoramic view of five nearby holes on the Sugarloaf golf course.

I wanted the house to be exquisitely furnished and decorated by the top professional interior decorators. Nothing but the best, including cutting-edge electronics, sound systems, home theaters—the works. Money was no object.

Now I also was able to cultivate my love affair with fine automobiles. After all, the driveway had to look as good as the house.

I decided to build my collection from what I had dubbed the "Big Three." Everything had to be top-of-the-line: a big luxury Mercedes S-Class sedan that would comfortably carry the entire family to our various outings, a tricked-out SUV with all the trappings for any overnight or weekend excursions, and of course, a really cool sports car—my personal favorite, a super-sleek silver Porsche twin turbo. It was amped up to 650 horsepower, with the Gemballa package and custom chrome wheels, including an upgraded, mind-blowing sound system. All my friends nicknamed it the Silver Bullet. Man, did that car turn some heads.

It was a far cry from the 1980 cream-colored Honda Accord that we bought after my rookie year with the Alouettes. Peggy had driven that thing until it was falling apart.

But new cars were only the beginning. I wanted us to dine at the fanciest restaurants and vacation at the ritziest resorts, including exotic locales such as Hawaii's Big Island and Atlantis in the Bahamas. I wanted to create memorable times for our family, making everything as special as possible when we were together.

The payoff for me was the expression of joy on my children's faces the first time they frolicked in the ocean with dolphins, stingrays, and other sea creatures.

Life was definitely good.

12
TRANSFORMATIONS

Through the end of 1997, the feud of the nWo faction versus the rest of the WCW was still going strong. The creative minds behind the story line made it edgy and cool, always mixing it up for the fans. Like many things in life, wrestling is cyclical, and keeping fan enthusiasm high is a challenge. I doubt that the WCW front office believed that the nWo story line would go on forever, and yet they were pleasantly surprised when it continued to generate ratings.

Still, you always have to be thinking about the next big thing. And what emerged from the nWo was unexpectedly big.

In May 1998, the nWo splintered into two rival factions: the nWo Wolfpac, led by Kevin Nash, against nWo Hollywood, led by Hogan. Everything about the babyface Wolfpac group just seemed to fall into place. A line from the theme song warned all opponents, "Don't turn your back on the Wolfpac," and fans certainly weren't—they were wholeheartedly embracing the new story line. T-shirts and memorabilia began flying off the shelves, and a few weeks after they came on the scene, I was fortunate to be wearing the new colors along with Sting.

Something else changed too. Earlier in the year, I began to incorporate the latest breakthrough in what were now called performance-enhancing drugs or PEDs. Composed of a weekly injection of testosterone along with a daily injection of human growth hormone (HGH) therapy, it would alter the world of professional sports forever.

This type of drug enhancement therapy wasn't only reserved for athletes. It was also being extensively utilized by the rich and famous as an antiaging therapy for both men and women, legally prescribed by endocrinologists. Testosterone and HGH naturally occur in our bodies, but after the age of thirty, the levels begin to steadily decline. So this type of replacement therapy is designed to bring the levels up to what they once were, reportedly giving a person more energy, a faster metabolism, and better muscle mass. It was touted by users as a veritable fountain of youth.

I was hoping it would make my steroid cycling obsolete; I liked the fact that I could stay on it year-round. Since it was legally prescribed, there would be no more worries about failing drug tests. And in addition to all the advertised benefits, I thought maybe it would help me with a nagging physical ailment that was becoming more pronounced.

■ ■ ■

From my high school days, I had always had a sciatica problem in my lower back. It had been diagnosed as spondylolisthesis of the L5, a condition in which one vertebra slides forward over the bone below it. I had lived with it, and obviously it didn't hinder my athletic performance.

Back in the mid-90s, I started experiencing a dull pain down my right hip when I was sitting on a plane, working out on the treadmill, or doing my back workouts.

It hurt, but I blew it off as my sciatica flaring up.

Finally, I consulted my orthopedic doctor about my recurring pain. When he looked at my back X-rays, he commented that it looked like there was an excessive amount of wear on my hips, which might be part of the problem. "You're probably going to need some work done on your hips."

"What do you mean by that?"

"Surgery."

"You've got to be kidding me."

"You're putting a lot of wear and tear on your hips from all your years of football, wrestling, and heavy leg presses and squats in the gym."

I thought he was crazy; I just had sciatica.

One morning when I was on the road having breakfast with another wrestler, I was feeling especially beat-up and road-weary, dreading my heavy leg workout. I pulled out a couple of Advil.

"Man, have you ever tried a painkiller with some coffee instead of the Advil?" he asked me.

"Why would I do that?"

"You'll feel like you could run through a brick wall at the gym."

"Really?"

I tried it, and it worked. I had the best heavy leg workout I'd had in a long time. From that point on, I added the combination of pills with coffee to my regular regimen before my workouts and matches, and I continued the ritual with my friends after matches, downing painkillers and muscle relaxers with alcohol.

■ ■ ■

We had wrapped another *Nitro* show, and I was ready to knock back a few with everyone. We kept beer on ice, ready to be cracked open after the show, with the pills divvied up among us. When I laid down the combination for Sting, he said, "No, thanks."

I looked at him. "What do you mean, no, thanks?"

"I'm not going to do it."

"Why aren't ya?" Sting had always been ready to party before. I thought he was joking around.

By this time, everyone else had stopped talking and was staring at us.

Sting's voice dropped, signaling me to leave it alone. "It's a long story, and I don't want to get into it now."

I could tell that my best friend was serious. Everyone else was wondering what was going on between us. To ease the tension, I made light of it. "No problem, I'll have yours, too," I said, downing his pills and mine.

I couldn't wait until we were alone, away from prying eyes and ears, to get the real story.

As soon as we got in the car to go back to the hotel, I asked him, "What's going on?"

"I'm thinking of asking for more time off, to spend time with my family. Lex, I feel like I'm drowning in drugs and alcohol. I'm losing my marriage and my family."

"Does that mean you can't drink a beer or pop a few pills with me? I won't tell anybody," I said sincerely.

"I made a commitment not to." He didn't elaborate any more than that.

Of course, I thought Sting was just going through a phase and that, sooner or later, he would be back doing pills and drinking with me. I thought, *He'll break down; he's my buddy.*

It never happened.

13
INJURY AND INTRIGUE

With a new year came another round of contract negotiations with the WCW, this time for a three-year deal and considerably more money. And then something unexpected happened.

I was in Los Angeles, California, on January 30, 1999, for a match. I had gone to Gold's Gym late in the day for a heavy biceps workout. Very early in the match, my opponent, Konnan, and I missed signals in the ring. He went one way, and I went the other. Suddenly, there was a pop, like a gun had gone off in the ring. It was so loud that the referee said, "What was that?"

None of us knew.

When the match was over, I knew that something wasn't right about my left biceps, even though it looked normal. Nothing hurt, but I knew my body well enough to realize that something was definitely wrong.

When I got home to Atlanta, I consulted various local doctors, but no one had an answer.

It was time to give Dr. Andrews a call.

When I saw him in Birmingham, he felt my arm and said, "Your biceps tendon is gone. I'll schedule you for surgery tomorrow."

Normally, when a biceps tendon snaps, your biceps muscle rolls up. But not in my case. The muscles in my forearm were holding my biceps in place, which is why the injury was nearly undetectable, stumping the Atlanta doctors.

It marked the first time in my thirteen-year wrestling career that I'd ever missed a match due to injury. I had been in probably close to four thousand matches, something I took great pride in. For me to be sidelined was big! Dr. Andrews said that the tendon needed at least four months to heal.

In many ways, it was perfect timing for me to be injured because the nWo Wolfpac story line had run its course and was winding down. When I came back, I planned to be in the best shape I had ever been in.

I did miss my after-match buzz, though. For the first time, I began to have a few beers and sneak pills at home before dinner, something I had never done before in front of my family. No one liked it, but my eight-year-old daughter, Lauren, was the most vocal about it.

"Alcohol isn't good for you," she'd say.

"Dad works hard," I'd tell her, "so it's okay for me to have a few beers." I teasingly nicknamed her the "beer police."

Out of the mouths of babes. But I wasn't heeding Lauren's warning.

■ ■ ■

It was time for a new story line for Lex Luger, one that I was familiar with from years before: The Narcissist. The inspiration was the introduction of tear-away athletic pants, a favorite apparel of professional basketball players. The pants, combined with a tear-away tank top, became my new costume.

I liked the tear-away costume, especially since it would give me the opportunity to again showcase my body, this time as a heel.

"Why don't we have one of the girls tear off your costume?" someone said.

"Yeah, why not have Miss Elizabeth do it?" suggested one of the bookers.

Having Elizabeth Hulette, who was considered the "first lady of wrestling," as my valet seemed to work for everyone. She had started in the business with the WWF in 1985, so she had a long history and appeal with the fans.

To create hype for the fall premiere, Elizabeth and I were filmed at a local funeral home, with me lying in an open casket and her dressed in black, mourning my death. (Many fans have asked me whether it was creepy being in a casket, but to be honest, it didn't bother me at all.)

On September 27, 1999, at the Philips Arena in Atlanta, Elizabeth walked onstage, dressed in a black trench coat and mourning veil. And then, out of the shadows, I appeared, back from the grave. It was the "rebirth" of Lex Luger.

Because of this new story line, I was now around Elizabeth more often. As can happen in any working relationship, the more time you spend with someone who has the same background and interests as you do, the more you get to know each other and can begin to enjoy each other's company. One day, early on, a friend of Elizabeth's mentioned that Elizabeth had a thing for me. Although it was intriguing, I didn't think very much about the comment at the time.

Not long afterward, I found myself involved in a full-blown extramarital relationship with Elizabeth, something I had vowed would never happen to me. I had always thought that messing around with someone at work was a toxic situation. So much for that self-declaration.

■ ■ ■

At first, I thought we were being discreet. After all, she lived in Miami, and I lived in Atlanta. Still, it wasn't long before people began asking me directly if I was having an affair with Elizabeth. I vehemently denied it.

"I'm a happily married man," I'd say. "We work together, but, no, we don't sleep together. We're strictly professional."

It should have been a big red flag to me when Elizabeth told me that she was moving to Atlanta. My good friend, Scotty Steiner, immediately saw where this was headed.

"That isn't cool that she's moving to Atlanta," he cautioned me. "She's got her eyes set on you, buddy. She wants to break up your family. That's going to be a disaster for you."

"No way. That isn't going to happen," I assured him.

In my mind, everything was under control.

When Elizabeth started showing up at my Main Event Fitness gym in Marietta with some of her friends, I took her aside.

"We can't see each other in Atlanta. This is where I live. This is where my wife and kids live," I explained. I rationalized that it was fine in work-related situations, but this was getting too close to home.

"I understand," she replied.

But the rumor mill wouldn't stop buzzing.

■ ■ ■

By late 1999, word about Elizabeth and me had finally gotten around to Sting. We were at a pay-per-view event, eating some catered food in the back prior to the match, when he confronted me.

"Hey, Lex, what are you doing, man?" Sting asked.

"What are you talking about?" I said, acting as if I didn't know what he meant.

"You and Elizabeth," he shot back.

"Oh, don't worry about it," I said.

"No, I *do* worry about it," he said. "I do worry because of Peggy, Lauren, and Brian. C'mon, Lex. You've got three people depending on you at home. What are you thinking?"

"Don't you worry about me, pally. There's plenty of 'The Total Package' to go around." I will never forget the look of disbelief on Sting's face when I said that. His jaw dropped, and he was temporarily at a loss for words.

That was okay with me. I didn't want to hear any more. I jumped out of my chair and quickly walked away.

How dare he lecture me! I had heard that Sting's brother was a pastor and that Sting had become a "born-again" believer. I had no idea what that meant, but I was angry. We weren't hanging out anymore. He had stopped doing the things we used to do together and going to the same places we used to frequent. He had gone religious on me. I felt like I had lost my best friend, and I was mad.

■ ■ ■

More and more, I did believe that I was "The Total Package." What had been a role for me had begun to work its way into my psyche. It was becoming my life.

Each and every morning, the first thing I did when I got out of bed was stand shirtless in front of a mirror, admiring myself and flexing my muscles. But it didn't stop there.

Before I'd get in my car, I would always stop and check out my reflection in the tinted windows of my Porsche. I loved what I saw so much, it was hard to tear myself away.

On a couple of occasions, when different friends shopped with me, I'd abruptly stop in front of a store.

After I had done this several times, someone finally asked, "What are you looking at?"

"Something incredible in the window."

Yeah, I was looking at something incredible in the window all right: me. I enjoyed looking at what I believed to be a perfect physical specimen.

From the meticulously coordinated Adidas and Nike sports outfits, to the custom-made clothes, to the specific color highlights I had running through my hair, to my bronzed tan, everything had to be perfect.

It all fit into my master plan. Although I loved my job, I had always seen professional wrestling as a means to an end. I planned to use my wrestling platform to launch a chain of Main Event Fitness gyms around the world. I would develop my own nutrition line and become the poster boy for a healthier lifestyle for baby boomers. In the wrestling world, I would be like Magic Johnson, Michael Jordan, and George Foreman combined—someone who would build a business empire after his sports career was over. I was convinced that the land of milk and honey was never going to stop flowing.

14
"CELEBRATING" MY SUCCESS

As the Monday night wars continued, WWF talent on *Raw*—such as Triple H, Shawn Michaels, the Undertaker, "Stone Cold" Steve Austin, and a new superstar, The Rock—were surging ahead of *Nitro*. To counteract this, the WCW had enticed Vince Russo to leave the WWF in 1999 as "head writer" and become an idea maker for us. In 2000, Russo and Eric Bischoff created a fresh stable of wrestlers— The New Blood—who began feuding with the established stars, dubbed the "Millionaire's Club." It was traditional in pro wrestling for established stars to help promote and validate new, exciting talent, endorsing them as the stars of tomorrow. Unfortunately, for whatever reason, the fans weren't buying this story line the way we had hoped. Meanwhile, the WWF's ratings continued to surge.

In January 2000, AOL purchased Time Warner, which had acquired Turner Broadcasting System (including the WCW) in 1996. Behind the scenes, I had heard the rumor that the powers that be at

AOL-Time Warner considered professional wrestling to be the black sheep of the company—and if there was any dip in our ratings, we'd be off the networks.

My suspicions were confirmed at a huge get-together at Turner Field after the announcement of the sale. This elegant catered lunch was a chance for all the top executives and top advertisers to reveal the long-range vision of programming for TNT and TBS for the decade to come. I had been invited to be there, too, to sign autographs— probably because we were still doing pretty well in the overall ratings. A lot was said that day, but pro wrestling was never mentioned.

When I got home, I told Peg that professional wrestling wouldn't be part of the company much longer. I believed the corporation was waiting for just the right moment, and we'd be gone.

As our ratings continued to slide and Vince's WWF ratings continued to rise, that moment came. We were sold to our competitor in March 2001. Vince McMahon had it all. He had won the Monday night wars.

Most people were shocked at the news. It was an incredible opportunity and a brilliant business transaction for Vince. He now owned almost all the archived material from the world of professional wrestling, along with most of the WCW talent. What he didn't have was the WCW large-contract talents; wrestlers like me weren't a part of the deal. We were independent contractors who had negotiated multiyear guaranteed contracts with AOL-Time Warner. The dream matchups that the fans had been anticipating wouldn't be happening anytime soon. The following year the WWF changed its name to World Wrestling Entertainment, Inc., shortened to WWE, which is its name to this day.

As for me, I thought the merger was fabulous. I came up with a new five-year plan for 2001 to 2006. For the next two years, I would be fully paid under my guaranteed contract, so I could focus on the development of my fitness and nutrition business. By not having to travel, I could stay home and focus on my training and eating—and hopefully put on about thirty pounds of solid muscle. I was excited! Just when the fans thought The Total Package couldn't get any better, I would be bigger and better than ever for my return to wrestling, ready for one final three-year run. I felt it would cap off two decades of wrestling excellence, leading to the launch of my fitness and nutrition empire.

■ ■ ■

In the summer of 2001, Peg and I decided to enroll our son, Brian, in Pace Academy, a private school on the northwest side of Atlanta, not too far from Main Event Fitness. He was developing into quite the high school basketball player. As a freshman in public school, he had started on the varsity team. By the end of that year, he was already six feet five and growing. We thought sending him to Pace Academy would be the best for him both academically and athletically. Peggy and I decided to rent an apartment for him close to campus so we wouldn't have to make the commute to school every day in the legendary Atlanta traffic. I would stay with him from Monday through Thursday, then we'd both return home to Sugarloaf for the weekend.

These new circumstances gave me more family time, as well as focused time at the gym—which also meant more time with Elizabeth, who lived near the gym. How convenient.

It also gave me time to work on my blossoming drug and alcohol consumption. Why not? I didn't have to punch a time clock or go to work anywhere. Before eating a nutritious breakfast, I would spike my OJ in the morning with a little vodka and some pills to start the day off with a light buzz. I would then get caffeined up for my grueling midday workouts at the gym, celebrating afterward with a few beers and pills with Elizabeth to catch another light buzz before I ate. All of this led up to the big buzz in the evening. Since Brian wasn't getting home for dinner until seven thirty at night, that meant I had a long happy hour. *You deserve it*, I'd say to myself. *You've worked hard all these years.* Why not celebrate my success?

That also meant developing my passion for spending money.

I remember stopping at an ATM to withdraw a couple grand so I could maintain my daily cash stash. I happened to glance at the balance on the receipt. There was over $700,000 just sitting in my checking account. Make more, spend more.

I was finding more creative ways to spend the money that was coming in.

One Christmas Eve I was doing some last-minute shopping in a jewelry store in Roswell, Georgia. It was after closing hours, but the store had stayed open for one other customer—Atlanta-based R & B crooner Usher—and me.

We nodded at each other but didn't really talk much as we scoured the expensive merchandise. It took me only an hour to drop about fifty grand in there. What fun! When it came to buying stuff, I felt like it was Christmas year-round.

■ ■ ■

The small hole that I had created in the fire wall between my family and my secret life was getting increasingly larger. The fact that my business was close to Elizabeth's apartment was a great cover. I certainly did spend time at the gym training and checking on the business side of things, but I also made time for Elizabeth. However, we weren't being as discreet as we had been in the beginning.

Sometimes after my midday workout, when I knew Brian was at school, Elizabeth would stop over at the apartment, and we'd catch a buzz together before eating. One afternoon, I heard Brian's key in the door, and my heart raced. *Why is he home early?* I scrambled and rushed Elizabeth into the closet in the spare bedroom where I slept.

I tried to act nonchalant, until Brian told me that he didn't have practice, so he was home for the rest of the day. *Oh, no!* To calm my nerves, I started catching a light buzz. *If worse comes to worst, Elizabeth will have to stay in the closet until Brian goes to bed*, I thought.

A few hours later, I suggested to Brian that we should get some carryout for dinner, hoping he'd go with me. He did. While we were gone, Elizabeth quickly slipped out.

After that close call, I admonished myself for being so careless. I vowed to be more cautious. That didn't last long.

■ ■ ■

We started off 2002 with a big birthday surprise for Brian. He was turning sixteen, and I had the perfect gift waiting for him in the garage on New Year's Eve—a beautiful black Escalade, topped with a giant red bow. At the stroke of midnight, I opened the garage door. It was a wonderful moment for all of us as we celebrated together.

February 14, 2002, was a day that would haunt me for years to come. Elizabeth had asked me for a ride to the nearby Range Rover dealership to drop her car off for some work. Before we left, she surprised me with Valentine's gifts. I left them sitting on the kitchen table, thinking that I would stash them when I got back in a few minutes. Brian was at school, and Peggy and Lauren never stopped by the apartment during the day, so it seemed safe.

Unbeknownst to me, while I was down the street with Elizabeth, Peggy stopped by the apartment with a surprise for Brian and me—a special Valentine's dinner she had prepared for us. Instead, she was the one who was surprised. Elizabeth's purse and her gifts to me were in plain sight on the table.

Whatever suspicions Peggy might have had over the years about me and my infidelity, the evidence was suddenly right in front of her eyes. I was irrefutably busted.

On the way back from the dealership with Elizabeth, my cell phone started ringing over and over again. It was Peggy. I knew something was wrong. I didn't answer the phone, but waited for it to go to voice mail. When I listened to her message, my heart was in my throat. Peggy was calling from the apartment. *What are you going to do now, Lex?* I thought.

I immediately turned the car around, dropped Elizabeth back at the dealership, and then headed to the apartment. I spotted Peggy's car. I didn't know what I was going to say yet, so I waited until she left for home. I knew she'd have to leave eventually, because Lauren would be getting home from school.

I spent that afternoon in a quandary. I decided that in this case, honesty would be the best policy. I would come clean—sort of.

I called Peggy that afternoon and explained to her how sorry I was that she had found those gifts in the apartment. I told her that even though Elizabeth and I didn't work together anymore, we still bumped into each other at the gym and had remained friends—and hung out together sometimes.

"Elizabeth had asked for a ride to her car dealership today. I was just helping her out. I was surprised when she brought me those gifts. And I'm so sorry that you found them there in the apartment.

"I love you, Peg. Can you please forgive me? For the sake of our family, for our children, please give me a second chance." I promised to immediately break things off with Elizabeth, assuring Peggy that our friendship was over.

As hurtful as that debacle was, Peggy decided to give me a second chance.

I lied once again.

I told Elizabeth that we could not be seen in public anymore. It was too risky. She needed to get an extra phone for me to use to call her. That way, our calls would appear on her phone bill, not mine.

As always, Elizabeth was cooperative and said she understood. We still saw each other at her apartment after my workouts and talked regularly on the secret phone.

■ ■ ■

It was the summer of 2002. At the end of the school year, we had given up the apartment on the west side, since Brian no longer needed it. He and I were both living at Sugarloaf now, and I had to start rushing back and forth again, commuting from our home to the gym every day.

I still believed I had it all together.

One summer morning, I hurriedly backed out of my driveway at Sugarloaf. I raced down the interstate in my Silver Bullet, zipping my Porsche in and out of traffic as I flew through Gwinnett, DeKalb, Fulton, and Cobb Counties as if my life depended on it.

It was like I was playing a video game. As I got to my exit, I was totally oblivious to the black, unmarked Suburban that followed me off the highway. Pulling into the parking lot of my destination, I relaxed. I had gotten there in record time!

That was when I saw the blue light on the dash of the Suburban. *Uh-oh.* A man dressed in street clothes got out of the car and approached my window. He looked at me and said, "Lex, where's the fire? You were doing 167 miles per hour. Why on earth were you driving that fast?"

I paused for a second before answering.

"I have a tanning appointment here," I confessed. "This place is always booked, and if I don't make it, it'll be forever before I can get back on the schedule."

Man, the look on his face. I realized that he was probably a detective. "Are you kidding me?"

"No, I have to keep my tan for the fans."

He shook his head in disbelief. "Lex, I'm going to pretend I never bumped into you. Promise me one thing, though. You're going to slow this thing down. Do you know how many people you endangered, including yourself?" Amazingly, I didn't get a ticket that day;

he let me go. The absurdity of my story caught him so completely off guard that he knew no one could make something like that up.

The more ridiculous my life became, the more I tried to rationalize my behavior as perfectly normal.

■ ■ ■

I decided I still needed a residence closer to my business. I didn't think it was unusual for a successful businessman who works in a large city to get a place in town closer to his office, while maintaining a family home in the suburbs. So I decided to have a secret town house built on the west side of town. It seemed logical to me, but I knew Peggy wouldn't go along with the idea. I had to keep it under wraps.

Keeping it a secret financially was no problem. I could have my private banker handle all that.

Even though juggling the east side/west side commute was stressful at times, everything seemed to be under control and going according to my plan.

In December 2002, Sting called me. Over the years since our blowup, he had continued to call on occasion and try to reach out to me, in spite of my hard feelings toward him. He said he was going on a two-week European tour with World Wrestling All-Stars (WWA), and one of the other main-event wrestlers had dropped out at the last minute. "Are you interested in filling his spot?"

"Yes, that would be great."

Actually, it didn't turn out to be great at all. I wasn't feeling well before I left, and once I got there, I was sick as a dog. I had pneumonia and was able to wrestle in only a few matches.

While I was gone, unbeknownst to my private banker, the final paperwork for the secret town house had been sent to my home address at Sugarloaf instead of to him.

Peggy was waiting for me with the paperwork in hand when I returned home.

"What's this? Why are we finalizing the closing of a town house in Cobb County?" she demanded. "What's going on?"

I was caught red-handed. I scrambled for an explanation. I decided to plead insanity.

"I'm sorry. I thought we needed to have a place closer to the business. I meant to tell you once things were finalized. Maybe the drugs and alcohol are affecting my decision making more than I thought. Maybe I do need some help," I told her.

I sat down with her and the kids and said I would go to the Ridgeview Institute in Atlanta for drug rehab.

In reality, I had no intention of getting help. I was just going to go to the town house to lay low, get high, and regroup.

I stopped answering phone calls from all my friends and family members. My life had become a total lie.

15

"I CAN'T BELIEVE THIS IS HAPPENING!"

My resolution for 2003 was to clean up my act. I didn't need to go to rehab—I would fix myself. I planned to stop drinking and taking pills in the mornings and afternoons, and just catch a light buzz before dinner. I vowed to myself that I'd get things back under control. After all, when I decided to do something, I always got it done. I would get in tip-top shape by the summer. The over-the-top celebration was over; it was time to get back to work.

Peggy was well aware that I hadn't gone to Ridgeview like I had promised her and the kids. By this point, mere words wouldn't even come close to making things right again. I wanted to get back on track; maybe, over time, my actions would speak louder than words. I assumed I wouldn't be welcome back at Sugarloaf anytime soon, so I decided to stay at the town house and be closer to the gym.

One day, Sting called to say he was in town and wanted to see me. When he came by, he pleaded with me to go back home, saying it was the right thing to do. Although I appreciated him coming by, I had no plans of taking his advice. It fell on deaf ears.

Of course, I wasn't totally alone on the west side of Atlanta—something I'm sure Peggy was aware of as well. One day a friend of Elizabeth's stopped by my town house; she was worried about Elizabeth's drug and alcohol intake.

The previous six months, there had been signs of Elizabeth increasing the amounts she needed for a buzz, but to be quite honest, I was too focused on myself to think of what was happening to her. As we talked, her friend's concerns brought some things to light.

"Lex, did you ever notice how accident-prone Elizabeth has been lately?"

"Yeah, but she always blames it on Sadie, saying Sadie jerked the leash when they were on a walk and pulled her down." (Sadie was Elizabeth's German shepherd.)

After talking about the situation, Elizabeth's friend and I both believed that drugs and alcohol were the more likely culprits. As I reflected on it, I knew she wasn't fine. She was coming to the gym less and less often, saying she didn't feel well. That wasn't like her. *She's not taking care of herself,* I thought.

Although I thought she was being a busybody, I told Elizabeth's friend that I would talk to her about it. And I did.

When I next saw Elizabeth, I said, "You know, I think we both need to clean it up a little more. Maybe cut back on the alcohol and pills." She nodded in agreement.

I needed to heed my own advice about cleaning things up. In early spring, I was involved in a fender bender on my way home from picking up some carryout. Nobody was hurt, but the police were called. I had had a few beers and pills before I left the house, so I did have an anxious moment when I was given a Breathalyzer test. But I passed with no problem. After I received a citation for the accident, I went on my way, feeling like I had dodged a bullet.

Brian's Siberian husky, Zoe, was now living with me at the town house, which was great company for Sadie. I had a fenced-in yard, and the two dogs loved playing with each other. One evening while Elizabeth and I were both catching a buzz, she announced that she wanted to take the dogs for a walk.

"Why don't you just let them out back?" I said.

She enjoyed walking the dogs, so she ignored my comment and began leashing them. I walked out into the garage to see them off, with no intention of going along. About ten feet down the driveway, the two dogs began romping after each other, and their leashes wrapped around Elizabeth's legs. She became hog-tied and fell down on the driveway hard, hurting her arm and shoulder and scraping her face under her right eye. It all happened in an instant. When I ran over to help her up, she insisted she was fine. We went inside and put a bag of ice on her eye. She was concerned about the scrape, so I suggested putting some Neosporin on it.

A few days later, we had both gotten buzzed before going to our favorite pizza place to pick up dinner. When we got home and I pulled into the garage, Elizabeth got out of the Porsche with the pizza box still on her lap, lost her footing, and stumbled. The pizza box flipped open, and the extra-large pizza loaded with everything went all over the inside of the car. She got up and began heading inside the town house.

I was definitely upset. "Hey! We need to clean this mess up now!"

"You clean it up!" she responded.

When she headed for the door that led into the house, I blocked her way.

We continued to argue, and Elizabeth kept trying to get past me into the house. As our voices got louder, a neighbor called the police.

We were both in the house when several squad cars pulled up. I opened the door. One officer asked me to wait outside while he talked to Elizabeth. I didn't think much of it, standing outside and chatting with the other policemen.

A few minutes later, the officer came back out through the garage. "Lex Luger, you're under arrest for domestic abuse." *What?* I was stunned. I had never laid a hand on a woman in my life. I was read my rights and taken to Cobb County Jail.

I was allowed my one phone call, which I made to my lawyer at 5 a.m. on Easter morning. He came down to the station, posted bond, and bailed me out. It was then that I learned the details of the charge. The arresting officer had seen Elizabeth's black eye and the abrasion on her cheek and believed that I had harmed her. Elizabeth had emphatically insisted that I had never touched her, and she was very upset that the officer had arrested me. The charges were eventually dropped, and at least for a few weeks, everything was back to normal.

■ ■ ■

Even though things were still tenuous between Peggy and me, she wanted our kids to have some kind of relationship with their father. She had begun bringing Lauren by the town house, and we talked about doing that at regular intervals. As for Brian, he had grown into a talented six-feet-eight junior power forward who was looking ahead to his senior season of high school basketball. He had blossomed into one of the area's top recruits and was receiving interest from a lot of major college programs.

May 1 was the last day of the open recruiting period when college coaches could come see him perform as a junior. A bunch of Division I coaches were scheduled to be at his school to watch him scrimmage and talk with him afterward. I was thrilled when Brian decided that he wanted me to be there to meet with them and help look out for his best interests.

That day I had a good workout at the gym, went home, showered, and then went to Pace Academy to meet Brian. Fortunately, I had been sticking to my game plan of staying straight during the daytime hours, which was a good thing because I wanted to be at my best in front of Brian and the coaches.

Before I left, Elizabeth had stopped by the town house and asked if she could hang out there while I was gone.

"Sure," I said. "I don't know when I'll be back. Probably not until at least dinnertime."

"That's okay," she said. "I'll see you later. Enjoy your time with Brian."

■ ■ ■

I didn't get home until around nine o'clock that evening. Elizabeth seemed to be somewhat high when I found her sitting downstairs in the home theater.

"I'm going to run over to Blockbuster and grab some movies," I said, ready to relax for the evening. To be honest, I was ready to get buzzed myself, then enjoy one of my favorite Boston Market meals: meat loaf and mashed potatoes.

When I got back from Blockbuster, I popped in an Arnold Schwarzenegger action flick. We partied with a few pills and cocktails but kept it light. I was talking about Brian and the scouts, and Elizabeth was happy that I had had the opportunity to be there.

I was really into the movie, but I did notice that Elizabeth kept dozing on and off. She'd wake up during the loud action scenes, then close her eyes again. I didn't think too much of it; since it was late, I figured she was tired.

By the time the movie was over, I was starving and decided it was time to microwave our meat loaf and potatoes.

Elizabeth was hungry as well, so she got up from the couch and walked over to the microwave to help.

"Go ahead and sit down," I said. "I'll bring it over to you."

I took her plate over to her on a tray, then sat back down on the couch and started digging into my dinner. She had taken a few bites of food, but the next moment I looked over, her head was rolled back as if she were sleeping.

"Hey, Liz, wake up!" I said. "Your food's getting cold!"

She didn't answer or move.

I said it again, a little bit louder. "Hey, Liz, let's eat!"

There was no response.

I set my tray aside, walked over, and knelt down in front of her, moving the tray off her lap. I nudged her, but she didn't move. *Man, she's really out!* I nudged her once again on her shoulder. She made a gurgling noise and some saliva came out of the side of her mouth, but she didn't open her eyes.

Something's not right!

When she didn't open her eyes, I decided to gently pull up one of her eyelids. I was immediately startled. Her eye was completely dilated. Something was terribly wrong. I could feel it in my gut. I ran to my phone and dialed 911.

"I need some help here now!" I screamed at the dispatcher.

The fire station was just down the road, so I knew the paramedics would be here in minutes, but I was still panicking.

"Is she breathing?" the dispatcher asked me.

"I don't know!"

"Do you know how to do CPR?"

"I took a course a few years ago, but I don't know if I remember how."

"I'll talk you through it," the dispatcher said, keeping me as calm as possible. "First, you need to lay her down on a flat surface."

I picked Elizabeth up off the couch and placed her on the floor. She was limp, like a rag doll. That really freaked me out.

I was frantically trying to blow air into her mouth, following the dispatcher's instructions as closely as I could, but Elizabeth wasn't responding.

Thankfully, I heard a knock at the door. *The paramedics!* I immediately let them in and took them to where Elizabeth was lying. They quickly put an oxygen mask on her face, then opened her blouse and began hand-massaging her chest, over her heart. I got out of their way, figuring that everything they were doing was normal. *She's in good hands now*, I thought. *She'll be okay.*

"We're going to have to transport her to the hospital," one of the paramedics said. As they put Elizabeth on a gurney and wheeled her out to the ambulance, I still wasn't aware of how critical her condition really was. I followed them outside.

There were emergency responders everywhere I looked. It seemed as if every cop and fireman in Cobb County were arriving on the scene. A big crowd was gathering.

As the paramedics closed the back of the ambulance, I said, "Should I hop in with you guys?"

One of them replied, "No, just meet us there." Then, with lights and sirens going, the ambulance left.

I started to head back inside to get my keys when I was stopped by a police officer. "You can't go back in there right now," he said.

"I need to get my car keys!"

"We can't let anyone back in the town house right now. We need to keep this area clear," the officer informed me.

I sat down on the front steps for a short while, but my patience ran out. No one was saying anything to me. I just wanted to get to the hospital.

I asked again, "Can I go inside and get my car keys?"

The officer said that no one could go inside.

I demanded to know why. "What's going on here? Why can't I go back inside?"

One of the lead cops took me aside. "Lex, I'm sorry. She didn't make it. She died on the way to the hospital."

What did he say? Elizabeth's dead?

I suddenly felt very light-headed, like I was going to pass out. I couldn't stand up anymore. I slid down the side of my town house and collapsed on the grass, my face buried in my hands. The impact of what had just happened started to hit me.

I can't believe this is happening! I kept saying to myself over and over. *How can this be happening?*

I asked the officer, through my tears, "Could you please give me a few minutes alone?"

I remember feeling hot, sweaty, and dehydrated.

After a few minutes, the same police officer came back. "Lex, we can't let you back inside, so let me take you down to the station where it's air-conditioned and I can get you something cool to drink. You don't need to be sitting here in front of all these people." It was turning into a real mob scene around me.

"When we get to the station, we'll go over what happened. It's all standard procedure."

16
AN UNEXPECTED TWIST AND TURN

At the Marietta police station, the detective and I went over the series of events that led up to the 911 call. Then we took a break.

When the detective came back into the room, he said, "I wanted to let you know that the medical examiner's preliminary findings indicate that Elizabeth died from an accidental overdose. We're pretty much done here, Lex. Who can I call to come pick you up?"

I gave him the name and number of a friend.

"Okay. I'll be back," he said, leaving again.

It seemed like a long period of time passed before the detective returned.

"Has my friend arrived?" I asked.

"Yes, he's waiting outside."

"Can I go now?"

"I have a few more questions to ask you."

WRESTLING WITH THE DEVIL

"Okay."

"Lex, sometimes these situations can take a twist and a turn."

I looked at him, thinking, *What does he mean by that?*

"Is there anything in your town house that you can think of that shouldn't be there?"

"No, not that I can think of."

"Are you sure about that?"

"Yeah, I'm sure."

"Lex, I want you to think about this carefully."

My mind was racing, but I couldn't think of anything illegal back in the town house. *What could they have found? Where's he going with this?*

"Lex, the guys on the scene did find something. Do you have any idea what that might be?"

I was honestly drawing a blank. "No, I don't."

"Lex, we found a considerable amount of anabolic steroids on the premises."

"That's news to me," I replied. "I have testosterone and human growth hormone at home, but I have legal prescriptions for those."

"That's not what I mean. We did a thorough search of your town house and found steroids."

"Where did you find that?"

"I really can't elaborate at this point. Unfortunately, here's the next step. The guys who conducted the search are here, and they're going to have to take you to the Cobb County Jail and book you on drug charges."

"You've got to be kidding me."

"I'm sorry. I wish I was."

Two detectives from the Georgia Bureau of Investigation (GBI) escorted me to their car. Ironically, both of them happened to be regulars at my gym. As we rode from the Marietta police station to the Cobb County Jail, they told me that the steroids had been found in a black gym bag in an upstairs bedroom closet; the vials were wrapped in electrical tape, unopened. *The spare bedroom!* That's when it hit me. Back in 1998 when I started going on the testosterone and the HGH therapy prescribed by my endocrinologist, I had stopped using anabolic steroids. But at the time, I had just received a shipment of them from Europe. Since I wasn't using them anymore, I threw the heavily taped package into a zippered pocket in a gym bag, instead of throwing it away. Everything in that spare bedroom closet had been shipped over from Sugarloaf, and I hadn't had time to go through it yet. How ironic that I was being arrested for possessing steroids that I hadn't used for years.

By the time we arrived at the jail, I was sleep deprived, exhausted, and totally drained. I was in complete shock—physically, mentally, and emotionally spent—when they locked me up.

I felt a sense of darkness and despair surrounding me in that cell, something that I had never experienced before. My entire world had come crashing down around me.

Before that moment, I'd always wondered how people could ever think about killing themselves.

But now I knew exactly how someone could get to that point. I felt totally alone, nearly smothered by a sense of utter hopelessness. I remember looking around and seeing the privacy wall separating the toilet from the rest of the cell and contemplating how I could end it all. *Maybe if I climb up on that wall and fall face-first with my hands behind my back, I could smash my skull and kill myself.* Then I realized, *Maybe the wall isn't high enough for me to finish the job.*

Fortunately, my lawyer, John, quickly bonded me out of jail and checked me into a nearby hotel, away from the media storm that had camped outside my town house.

He instructed me that it would be best to stay at the hotel for the next couple of weeks and keep a low profile.

■ ■ ■

It rained for the next two weeks. The miserable weather reflected my mood. I had been at the hotel a few days when I started going a little stir-crazy, so one evening I decided to walk downstairs to the lobby. As I passed the bar, I glanced at one of the television screens and did a double take. It was footage of me; I was still a headline story being covered on the local news. I turned around, went back to my room, and locked the door, never venturing out again for the remainder of my stay.

I didn't have to worry about getting drugs and alcohol; a friend would periodically drop them off, keeping me well supplied. I stayed high and intoxicated for the next two weeks.

During this time, I completely shut myself off from everyone, with two exceptions—my lawyer, John, and Sting. The day I called Sting, I'm pretty sure I was high because I don't remember anything I said to him. I didn't talk to any of my family; I just wanted everyone—and everything—to go away. I didn't read any newspapers or watch any of the local or national news shows.

As the two weeks came to an end, I made it clear to John that I didn't want to go back to the town house. He had been talking with some friends of mine from the gym, and everyone agreed that it was best for me not to. Instead, they found me a condo in Buckhead that I could move into when I left the hotel.

John apprised me of everything that was happening with my case. I was being charged with multiple counts of felony drug possession, but it was going to be a while before this went to trial.

"Time is on our side," he kept reassuring me. "By the time this gets through the legal system and with you being a first-time offender, I'm optimistic that, in the end, it won't turn out as badly as it seems."

He did have some bad, albeit not surprising, news. Peggy had filed for divorce soon after I moved to Buckhead. He promised to take care of everything with that, too.

"Hang in there. Don't worry about anything," John said. "Start going back to the gym, take care of yourself, and keep a low profile."

I did start going to the gym again. But the rest of John's advice? I let it go.

Everyone thought this was going to be a wake-up call for me, but I went in the opposite direction.

■ ■ ■

Buckhead was the happening place to be in Atlanta at the time. I had never been a part of the club scene in Atlanta before; I had specifically avoided that. But now my double life had been totally exposed. Why keep up the pretense? I began acting out—livin' large—going to nightclubs and all the local hot spots in my flashy cars. I was the celebrity "bad boy" that our pop culture always embraces, the one everyone wants to hang out with.

Our divorce was finalized in November 2003, a few weeks before our twenty-fourth anniversary.

By the end of the year, I was getting tired of the partying crowd in the clubs. I came to the realization that those types of people are partying *on* you, not *with* you. They only like you because you give them access to VIP rooms and pick up the tab. So I began hanging out at the condo with friends, people that I thought really cared about me. Some certainly did—like my sister, Barbara. I would invite her and her family over for barbecues fairly often, since they lived nearby.

■ ■ ■

After the divorce was finalized, I had hoped to reestablish a relationship with Peggy and the kids, but understandably, they were extremely reluctant.

The year 2004 became my year of the two-a-days. I started the routine of getting high in the morning before my pre-workout lunchtime meal. After that, I'd get caffeined up and go to the gym, and then get high again at night before a late evening meal.

People who saw me at the gym probably thought I was doing fine. But my friends who were privy to my behavior on the weekends at the condo saw a different Lex. Most of them were getting high with me. I did have a couple of friends who were concerned enough about me that they'd wait for me to pass out, then pour my vodka down the sink and flush my pills down the toilet before they left. When that happened, I'd have to replenish my stash. It became a back-and-forth game for us. But sometimes it actually would slow down my intake—at least for a while.

My family was very concerned. My mom called me regularly from Buffalo, and my sister called and visited. They knew I had a problem and did everything they could to help me. They were both my rocks that year.

I did succeed in staying out of trouble, because I was mostly hanging out at the condo watching movies with my friends. We certainly weren't hurting for movie choices. We had gone to the local Blockbuster, and I had practically bought out the entire store.

But I felt like I was in limbo, just waiting for things to move forward in my life. Whenever I asked John if anything was happening on the legal front, he kept telling me to be patient, not get discouraged, and keep it together—easier said than done.

My year of keeping it together was about to end.

17
GOING DOWN FAST

In January 2005, John called and said my legal case was finally going to be settled. We still didn't know for certain what the judge's final decision would be. I was excited but apprehensive at the same time. For two years, I had been carrying the weight of not knowing the outcome—would I be able to get back to my plan, or would I have to do jail time? In early February, the moment of truth arrived.

The judge gave me a five-year sentence; I was now a convicted felon. The good news was that in the state of Georgia a nonviolent, first-time offender could be given probation—it was totally up to the judge. When the ruling was made and I heard the word *probation*, I was so relieved, like a grand piano had been lifted off my back. While I was on probation, I would be required to do community service.

I was fired up. Now I could move forward with my life. It was time to hit the gym and get back to work.

The following week, while I was going through my mail, I saw a letter from Cobb County that I had missed a court date for one of my many traffic violations that had accumulated over the past couple of years. My driver's license was currently suspended, so I was hoping to clear this up and get it reinstated.

I was told to report to the Cobb County Jail to take care of the violation; otherwise, they would issue a warrant for my arrest.

I got a ride to the jail, and when I pulled out my credit card to pay the fine at the desk, the clerk kept typing on his computer. Then he said, "Do you have an outstanding warrant anywhere?"

"Absolutely not!" I said confidently, thinking everything would be all right in a few minutes.

"The computer says there's an active warrant issued for you in Gwinnett County, Georgia. Sorry, Lex, we're going to have to place you under arrest."

I couldn't believe it. After all that time anticipating staying *out* of jail, here I was going *to* jail.

The following day, my attorneys (John and a separate lawyer who had been handling all my traffic-related violations) explained to me what had happened. It had been a while since I had paid alimony and child support to Peggy and the kids. My plan was that once I got back to work, I would bring things up to speed. However, I hadn't informed the judge in Gwinnett County of my intentions, and he had issued the warrant. My lack of communication was obviously a huge mistake. I would have to spend the following seven to ten days in lockup until I was placed on the docket at the Cobb County Courthouse to settle my traffic violation. Then I would be extradited to the Gwinnett County Jail immediately afterward to be held, without bond, until my court date for the charges related to the missed alimony and child support payments.

For the first time, I was issued my very own Cobb County blue flannels and rubber sandals. I was placed in isolation for security reasons, due to my so-called celebrity status. When my day at

Cobb County Court arrived, I was transported in my blue flannels, restrained with wrist and ankle shackles. Traffic court was packed. I was brought in from a side door and was marched out in full display in front of the judge and the courthouse audience. It was definitely not the type of entrance I wanted to be known for. I'll never forget the looks of shock on everyone's faces. It certainly made their day in traffic court a memorable occasion.

I was taken back to Cobb County Jail, where I changed into my street clothes and waited to be picked up to go to Gwinnett County Jail. It was a Friday night when I arrived at Gwinnett, and the intake area was jammed—it was a full house. I spent the entire night in the holding area.

I was finally brought into the processing room, stripped naked in front of several officers and inmates, sprayed down with lice disinfectant, rinsed off, then handed green flannels and rubber sandals. It was an extremely embarrassing and humiliating moment. I remember thinking, *This is a long way from the VIP check-in at the Ritz-Carlton.* For the first couple of days, I was in the infirmary, where they could monitor me for any withdrawal symptoms from drugs and alcohol. Surprisingly, I didn't feel any major physical effects. I certainly craved them, but I didn't go through the typical withdrawal that most addicts experience. It made me feel as though I wasn't a true drug addict, that I was in control. Eventually, I was put in a small isolation cell for security reasons.

A short time later, I sat down with one of the officers, who explained my three options: (1) I could be placed in a cell by myself—twenty-four hours a day—with no interaction with other inmates; (2) I could share a cell with one other inmate and have very limited interaction with other inmates in a common area; or (3) I could share a cell with three others and be placed in the general population, with the least restrictions of all for the common area.

"What would you do?" I asked him.

"To be honest," he said, "twenty-four-hour isolation is rough, even for the most hardened criminals." He thought that because of my celebrity status the second option would be the best, but I chose the third option—general population. I had never liked being confined in small spaces. I wanted to have as much freedom of movement as possible. "Suit yourself," he said, "but be prepared. You're going to get swarmed."

I quickly learned from my 180 fellow inmates on my pod how things worked, especially the "monetary" system. As with most jails, every inmate could have a bank account to draw from. Friends or family would deposit money in the account, which an inmate could then use to buy snacks like candy bars, chips, or even cigarettes. My sister, Barbara, would make a weekly deposit for me for the maximum amount permitted. All of us inmates had individual storage bins in our cells, where we would store our "money"—the snacks or items we had bought or traded for other items. The two most valued food commodities inside the Gwinnett County Jail were instant cups of soup and honey buns. They were like gold. I'd stock up on my snacks in my "bank," first by purchasing them, then by working deals with other inmates who had run out of snacks for the week. We did what was called a two-for-one. For example, if you "borrowed" one from me one week, you'd "pay" me back with two the next week. My bin filled up fast.

But what I needed more than snacks was real food. I was taught by a cellmate how to barter for extra meals. If an inmate owed me, I'd sit across from him at mealtime. When I was done with my tray, he'd slide me his. After a couple of weeks, I was eating two portions at every meal. It was a matter of survival for me; my body was used to consuming huge amounts of calories at home. I was trying to hold on to as much size as I could.

I never had any problems with the other inmates. As my three other cellmates wisely told me at the outset, "Most of the guys in here just want to serve their time and get out. Just treat everyone with respect. If you mind your own business, they'll mind theirs. That's the best way to avoid being thrown in the 'hole.'" The "hole" was isolation, where you were sent for disciplinary reasons. Understandably, I got peppered with questions from the inmates about pro wrestling, but it did help kill the time.

Being incarcerated definitely makes you appreciate the simple things in life that most of us take for granted—like being able to do the things you want to do when you want to do them. Here, there was no such thing as privacy—everything was communal and out in the open, including going to the bathroom or taking a shower.

When my release from jail was finally arranged, almost two months had passed. (I would eventually meet with a judge regarding my case.) I was finally free. I just wanted to go home, take a nice hot shower, get buzzed, and then eat a double Whopper with cheese and McDonald's French fries.

■ ■ ■

It was good to be home and back to my familiar routine. Not that I had started doing things in moderation. Since my release, I was throwing caution to the wind when it came to getting high. One night I stumbled and hit my head on the granite kitchen countertop, gashing my forehead open between my eyes. I woke up the next morning in a pool of blood on the carpet. It looked like a crime scene. I thought to myself, *Wow, you must have really overdone it last night.* A friend took me to the emergency room to get stitched up. Obviously it didn't worry me too much, because I was right back at it that night.

Another time, a short while later, I was riding shotgun in my friend's pickup, on the way back from replenishing my supply of drugs and alcohol. I couldn't wait until we got back to the condo, so I started popping pills and drinking on the way home. Talk about fast and furious! I got buzzed so quickly that when we arrived and I stepped out of the truck, I fell onto the concrete and split the back of my head wide open. I refused to go to the hospital. I sat in my recliner, and my friends kept wrapping my head in towels, trying to stem the flow of blood. It eventually stopped, although I had throbbing headaches for weeks afterward, probably the result of a concussion. Neither of these incidents, nor other similar ones, slowed down my escalating consumption of drugs and alcohol.

Finally, my lawyers advised me that it was time to get busy and take care of all the community service hours I was obligated to fulfill. I was assigned to work at an animal shelter, which was at least a forty-five minute drive from where I was living in Buckhead. Without a driver's license, this commute was going to be a real pain, especially with Atlanta traffic. I had to go five days a week, starting in June.

We decided it would be best to find a temporary place for me to stay that was closer to the animal shelter, like a hotel where I could pay by the week. We found the perfect spot in Kennesaw, Georgia: an extended-stay hotel right by a Gold's Gym, the Toucan tanning salon, and Supplement Depot, a sports nutrition store. I couldn't believe it! Everything I needed to get back on track was lined up within walking distance of the hotel. And down the street was the Town Center Mall, which had plenty of restaurants.

I stored all my furniture and moved into the hotel. I kept it simple: I had a suitcase, a rack of clothes, and my big-screen TV.

■ ■ ■

Getting my community service behind me was going to be harder than it looked. I woke up early every weekday morning in order to get to the animal shelter on time for my ten-hour shift. There was no such thing as slacking off; I was being closely monitored. For the rest of the summer, I picked up poop, scrubbed and hosed down dog kennels, washed food dishes, and—worst of all—cleaned out cat cages. I did wear heavy gloves to protect myself from being scratched and bitten by the cats, but they always managed to leave their marks. They were a lot meaner than the dogs, hissing when I picked them up to disinfect their cages.

I also did the laundry and moved furniture in the offices—you name it, I did it. To make things worse, it was a *beastly* Hotlanta summer (no pun intended).

I've never worked that hard in my entire life. I was exhausted at the end of each day. When my friend would pick me up, he'd have a huge cup of iced lemonade mixed with vodka in one cup holder and my pills in the other. I'd unwind by getting high on the way home. It was difficult not being able to get high in the morning and staying sober all day, so I would get extra-high at night to make up for it. I always looked forward to the weekends, when I could get some extra rest and work out a little bit as well. I was too tired to do that during the week.

On top of everything else, my right hip was starting to bother me all the time. I had noticed it when I was released from jail. It seemed to get worse after a few weeks of working at the animal shelter, especially since I was on my feet all day. I kept telling myself that once things got back to normal with my regular workout routine, my hip would be fine.

■ ■ ■

Summers had always flown by for me before, but not this one. It dragged, and so did I. By August, I did something I had never done before—I stopped going to the gym altogether. Workouts had always been an integral part of my daily life.

At other times in my life, I had never allowed doubt and uncertainty to chip away at my confidence. I'd just push them aside.

Not this time. I was fighting discouragement at every turn. For the first time, I questioned my ability to accomplish my goals. It was *never* supposed to happen this way. I had planned to be wrestling by now.

I was becoming more and more isolated in that hotel room. My emotions were churning inside of me.

Off the coast of Florida, a tropical storm was starting to swirl as well. Hurricane Katrina was poised to make landfall and leave unbelievable destruction in its wake.

18

THE WAKE-UP DREAM

The television was tuned to Fox News for coverage of the hurricane. It was so depressing to watch, and the weather outside didn't help. The rain was coming down nonstop, obviously an effect of the storm that was pummeling Florida and the Gulf Coast.

It was a Friday night, and I was alone in Kennesaw, far away from everyone, isolated from friends and family. No one was there to hang out with me; there were no constraints. So I decided to go in really deep. I doubled up on everything.

I sat back on the couch and eventually passed out. And the dream began.

It was incredibly real and vivid—the colors were dazzling, the clouds were vibrantly white, with more definition than I had ever seen. The people and everything surrounding me were extremely detailed.

I slowly realized that I was lying in a casket with the top removed, set on the grass in a cemetery. All my family and friends were circled around the casket, and I could see them clearly. I did think it was odd that I was outdoors in an open casket, but I enjoyed looking at the sun and the beautiful clouds in the blue sky above. Based on the location of the sun, I figured it must be about 11 a.m. This seemingly perfect day was the day of my funeral.

Then something changed. I thought, *This is weird.*

I could still see the sky, but I wasn't in the casket anymore. I was suspended just beneath the surface of glistening, clear water.

Once again, I thought how strange this all was. *What is going on here?*

I began to drop slowly, still facing upward. Everything around me became darker and darker, colder and colder. It seemed like I was in an endless free fall. Deeper and deeper I went.

I didn't know what was happening to me, but I was definitely becoming frightened. It wasn't the fall itself that was terrifying me, but how deep I was going.

There was no sound whatsoever. I finally hit the bottom, on my back, my body settling into muck.

It was pitch-black and freezing cold. *There's no way out of here*, I thought. *It's too far up for me to swim back to the top.*

My worst nightmare was coming true—I had always felt that the worst way to die was drowning. You'd be conscious, trying to breathe. It would take time to die. Now I found myself in that exact predicament.

That's when it hit me. *I need to breathe.* But there wasn't any air to breathe down there. I desperately tried to hold my breath as long as I could to prevent the water from rushing into my lungs. My mind was racing; fear and panic set in. *What do I do? What do I do?*

Then I began reasoning with myself.

"Lex, just lie back. Let go. Don't fight it. Breathe in, and it will all be over. Just relax and breathe in that water."

In my mind, I could feel the weight of all my bad decisions—and their tragic consequences—pressing down on me.

"Look at what your life has become," I told myself. "Just breathe in that water, and you won't have to struggle anymore. If you don't fight it, everything will be over before you know it."

I could feel myself beginning to relax. I was starting to give in, realizing that my whole life had been nothing more than a pipe dream. *Is this all there is? You're born, you live, then you die in the darkness, all alone?*

I guessed it was true. "Lie back, Lex," I repeated to myself again. "Breathe it in."

But just as I was starting to let go, all of a sudden I felt a distinct presence down there with me. I didn't know what it was, but I instinctively knew where to look for it. It was above me and to my left.

The presence was undeniably real. Yet I was annoyed that it had disturbed me. I just wanted to lie back. But I couldn't let it go; I had to find out what it was.

With one last superhuman effort, I pushed with all my might. I fought to sit up in the muck, in hopes of seeing what had gotten my attention.

Suddenly, I saw it—a tiny white speck, the size of a pinhole in the vast darkness, giving the merest hint of the most brilliant white light I've ever seen. I was craning my neck toward that light, and when I did, I realized that the brilliance was outside of the darkness that was trying to engulf me.

What is that light? I wondered.

Whatever it was, it saved my life.

Just then, I realized what was happening and was terrified. My mind was racing, and my heart was pounding. *I've got to do something. I've got to get out of here.* The light seemed to empower me to fight back against the urge to let go.

When I awoke on the couch, I was sitting straight up, looking toward the ceiling. I had never felt such pure fear before, not even when I was in the motorcycle accident.

Without realizing what I was doing, I raced across the hotel room and opened the drawer of the nightstand next to the bed. I grabbed the Gideon Bible inside and stared at it for a minute. Then I opened it up and began reading a few verses. I had never read a Bible before. Then I thought, *Why am I doing this?* so I tossed it against the wall. Still, what I had read calmed me.

The next day I picked up the Bible again. I read through the first four chapters but got bogged down in chapter five by who was born and how long each person lived. I couldn't pronounce many of the names. *I don't understand this at all.*

There was something else I didn't understand. I had always been a sound sleeper and never remembered my dreams, except on rare occasions when I would recall a quick flash of what I had just dreamed. For the first thirty seconds after I woke, I might be able to describe one thing, but never an entire dream with the kind of detail that I had just experienced.

I am certain that I overdosed that night in the Kennesaw hotel room. I believe I went through a life-and-death struggle at the bottom of that pond and survived.

■ ■ ■

I had run out of pills; I had taken them all. When I called my drug supplier, I couldn't get through to him. *This is unusual,* I thought. *He always calls me right back.* What I didn't know was that he was in Florida and couldn't get a signal.

It was Sunday. I had no pills and no vodka, and I couldn't buy any.

I made the decision that I was going to ride things out. I wasn't going to leave that hotel room until my head was clear and my body was completely detoxed. I had scared myself straight—at least for the moment.

I began going to the gym twice a day and eating clean. I knew things had to change. I was determined to get in the best shape of my life.

Don't get me wrong: I hadn't decided to give up drugs and alcohol forever. I just knew I had to lay off them for a while.

Every month, I'd get my prescriptions filled and leave the newest full bottles of painkillers and muscle relaxers on display on the counter in front of an unopened bottle of vodka, to help reinforce my "mind over matter" challenge. I wasn't an addict. I was going to prove that point to myself and anyone who might question it.

When my drug dealer called me, I told him that I was working hard, getting ready for wrestling, and going straight for a while.

"I'm happy to hear that, Lex," he said. "I've been worried about you. You've been going through a lot of vodka and pills lately. I was getting concerned."

Okay, I did ask my dealer for some Deca and testosterone. When I combined those with my workouts over the next twelve weeks, my body exploded. I was big, muscular, and lean. I was thrilled. I felt my ninety-day extreme makeover was a rousing success.

19
MY LUCK
RUNS OUT

It was time to put myself back on display, to create a positive buzz through wrestling's independent circuit. My first choice was an operation based out of Winnipeg, Canada, which would involve two different appearances—one in a non-wrestling capacity in late October, and the other as my return to the ring for a wrestling debut in early December. My second choice was a regional independent in Rome, Georgia, an hour outside of Atlanta, a week before Christmas.

Everything went smoothly during my initial brief visit north of the border, and the return for my wrestling debut was greatly anticipated. It wasn't long before the big weekend arrived. I grinned with excitement as my plane landed at Winnipeg International Airport. Once again, everything was problem-free—until I handed the customs official my passport. When he ran my name through the computer, an active warrant for my arrest popped up for Cobb County, Georgia. I didn't see that one coming. I was promptly shuffled off to a private side room with my luggage in tow. The customs officials explained that I was going to be denied access to Canada because of my outstanding warrant. I spent the next few hours undergoing a very thorough strip search of my person and a detailed examination of all my belongings. Then I was escorted to the tarmac by two armed Canadian border patrol officers for a flight back to Atlanta, where Cobb County law enforcement would be waiting for me when I got off the plane. It wasn't a direct flight; my plane was making a brief stopover in Minneapolis before continuing to Atlanta. There went my much-anticipated wrestling debut.

I was extremely disappointed, but I figured that when I landed at the Atlanta airport, I'd turn myself in to the Cobb County police, then quickly bail myself out of jail before returning to the hotel to regroup.

I never would have guessed what was about to happen next.

When our plane rolled up to the gate in Minneapolis, I couldn't help but notice a large fleet of law enforcement vehicles on the tarmac, with lights flashing. I wondered what all the commotion was about.

I was seated about halfway down the aisle, in a row by myself. The passengers around me who needed to catch connecting flights began to stand up and get ready to deplane. Then the captain's voice came over the intercom. He asked everyone to please return to their seats and remain seated.

At that point, six of the biggest US customs agents I have ever laid eyes on boarded the plane and slowly began walking toward the back, staring straight ahead. One walked past my seat and continued on, followed by a second one who glanced over at me. I knew it right then. They were on the plane for me. A third agent walked past me. I was now surrounded—three men behind me and the other three in front of me.

One of the agents behind me tapped me on the shoulder.

"Is that your carry-on luggage?" he asked, pointing to the bag sitting at my feet.

"Yes, sir," I said.

"Do you have anything else?"

"No, sir."

They asked me to get up and began walking me down the aisle toward the exit. It must have been quite a sight for the other passengers to see a guy my size, wearing a sleeveless shirt, being slowly escorted off the plane by customs agents. I'm sure some of the other passengers were wondering if I was some kind of axe murderer being taken away.

Just outside the exit door, they stopped and handcuffed my hands and feet, then added one-piece reinforced cuffs on top of the standard cuffs to further restrain me. Now it was impossible for me to walk.

They had to carry me down the steps. It was frigid in Minneapolis, something like six below zero. When we got to the ground, they quickly shoved me into the back of a waiting black Suburban.

Once again, I had inadvertently created a scene. Passengers were peering out of the plane, and spectators inside the terminal were crowded by the windows, pointing in our direction. Inside, I was whisked off to a remote area of the airport, where the customs agents conducted a strip search on me and went through my bags thoroughly.

When the agents had finished combing through everything, they uncuffed me and turned me over to local authorities. The Hennepin County police handcuffed me once again and took me to the county jail, located beside the Target Center in Minneapolis, a place where I had wrestled many times before.

On the way to the jail, the local police officers told me they were surprised that the customs agents had taken me off the plane for a nonviolent criminal offense. As it turned out, the feds were practicing how to respond to a terrorism threat in an airport. They had taken the opportunity to use me as their guinea pig. Since I had an active warrant, they had every right to do so.

I arrived at the Hennepin County Jail and was placed in isolation for the first day. I asked to be placed in the general population the following day and immediately began "banking" so I could get extra food. I was detained in Minneapolis for two weeks before I was extradited back to Cobb County on December 21, 2005. I wanted to get back home as fast as I could to straighten this whole thing out. I figured I would definitely be out before Christmas.

■ ■ ■

It was already early evening by the time we landed in Atlanta. Once again, I had a welcoming committee ready to take me to the Cobb County Jail. By now, I certainly knew the drill. I learned that my arrest warrant was for not checking in with my probation officer. It hadn't been intentional. I was so busy getting ready for my debut in Canada that it had simply slipped my mind.

Because I had been up and traveling since 4 a.m., I wasn't in a cheery mood. I was exhausted. I was taken to my cell inside the infirmary for my routine physical. Just as the medical staff walked out and shut the door, I noticed a tall man walking up to the Plexiglas window of my cell.

He was carrying something.

"I'd like to speak with you for a moment," he said to me.

"What do you want?" I responded curtly. "I'm really not in the mood to talk to anybody." All I wanted to do was lie down.

"It will only take a moment. My name's Steve. I'm one of the jail chaplains."

"I don't care who you are," I replied. "I don't feel like talking right now."

"Well, can I at least give you this?" He started to hand me something through the food slot in the door, where the trays are passed through.

For a fleeting moment, I actually thought about slamming the slot door down on the guy's fingers, but I didn't. I snatched his gift without looking at it, threw it on the floor, then went back to my bed.

I didn't care that he was trying to be nice to me. And as for the gift? I didn't realize it was a Bible until the next morning.

20
A TRUE FRIEND
IN THE COBB COUNTY JAIL

I was transferred from the jail infirmary into a general population pod.

A few days later I appeared before the same Cobb County judge who had sentenced me originally. I was hoping to get home for the holidays. Unfortunately, it didn't go down that way. The judge showed me no leniency whatsoever. He explained that it was my responsibility to make all my monthly appointments with my probation officer; I had missed my last two. He also explained that as part of my probation, any time I left the state—or especially the country—I needed to have all my paperwork done properly, which I had not done for my trip to Canada. "Probation is a privilege, not a given," he sternly lectured me. "I'm going to give you four months in the Cobb County Jail with one month taken off for time served in Minneapolis. If I see you again, you will spend the remainder of your five-year sentence in our state prison system. Am I clear on that?"

"Yes, sir, Your Honor."

The Cobb County Jail was going to be my home for the next three months.

I appreciated the reduction for the time I had served in Minneapolis, but the news that I had to stay in jail for three months crushed me. To be honest, I wanted to get out of jail, go home, watch some football, and relax.

I had cleaned up my act; I thought I had turned things around. *So much for living right.* No more Mr. Goody Two-Shoes for me. I vowed from that moment to return to being the old Lex. It would be a whole lot easier.

That is, if I got through the next three months. Cobb County Jail was not designed with the word *fun* in mind. There were no TV privileges, and any available books had the story's ending page torn out by a previous reader just for spite. Apparently I wasn't locked up with a literature-loving crowd. And the fact that there wasn't a clock in sight made me feel like time was standing still.

What I did notice was that the jail chaplain who had given me the Bible was always knocking on the window of our pod whenever he came by. He'd smile and motion for me to come up to the door, but I'd always wave him off.

After weeks of this, it became a running joke among my cellmates every time he'd stop by. "Here comes that chaplain again, Lex!" they'd say. "He's going to try to get you to talk to him."

Finally one of them mentioned the advantages of taking the chaplain up on his offer: you could get out of the cellblock for a period of time. That would at least break up the monotony. *And maybe if I meet with him once, he'll go away,* I thought.

So the next time that chaplain walked by, I met him at the window, much to the astonishment of my cellmates. "What do you want?" I asked.

"I want to talk to you," he replied. "I can have the guards bring you to a room, and we can talk for a little bit."

Although I was skeptical about his intentions—I didn't want him to bombard me with religious talk—I agreed. After all, I figured that I could always walk out on him and be put back in my cell if the conversation became uncomfortable.

■ ■ ■

When we got to the room, he introduced himself to me again. "I'm Steve Baskin, one of the chaplains here." It was awkward at first, just a little get-acquainted chitchat. When he pulled out his laptop and turned it on, I thought, *Oh great, here it comes! Laying the religious stuff on me.*

Instead, it was an action movie.

"I know you can't watch TV in here, but we could watch a movie on my computer if you'd like."

I wasn't expecting that. "Nah, that's okay."

We talked a little longer, and then it was time for me to go.

"By the way," Steve said, "the food's pretty bad in here, isn't it?"

"Yeah. It's definitely bad, and it's not near enough. I feel like I'm starving all the time."

"Here, have a few of these," he said, handing me squeezable packets of peanut butter.

"Thanks! I really appreciate it." *This guy isn't so bad after all.*

A few packets of peanut butter might not seem like much to most people, but they were protein and sustenance to me. I began saving all the extra bread from my meals and trading for other inmates' bread so that I could make peanut butter sandwiches for my late-night snack. Steve began slipping peanut butter to me on a regular basis, even though he probably wasn't supposed to.

I had never talked to a pastor before and had preconceived notions about what a pastor was like. But I was pleasantly surprised. Pastor Steve was, well, normal—a regular guy with regular issues and challenges.

Over the ensuing weeks, I took every opportunity I could to meet with him and got to know him much better. We had a lot more in common than I ever would have thought. He grew up in California and had been an incredible high school athlete who had excelled in both basketball and track (he was a state champion in the high jump). But in college he decided that his calling was to become a pastor. For the past twenty years he had been pastoring a church, as well as being one of the jail chaplains at Cobb County.

The only subject we didn't touch upon was religion. What a relief! He was one of my only visitors other than my lawyer, my sister, and my nephew. Although our conversations had become a regular thing, I didn't plan on ever seeing him again once I got out of jail.

■ ■ ■

In March 2006, I was about to be released from the Cobb County Jail when Pastor Steve came by for the last time.

"You know, I've put on some pounds these last couple of years, and I've been meaning to get in shape. What do you think of us getting together at the local gym so you could help me with my workouts?"

"Sure, whatever, Pastor Steve," I said, not giving it a second thought. I wasn't a personal trainer; I only trained myself. I didn't give him my address or phone number or the name of the gym I usually went to. *Good luck finding me.*

A friend picked me up from the jail with just what I needed to restart my old life—my spiked Arnold Palmer (half iced tea and half lemonade) in one cup holder and my pills in the other. I was on my way back to the extended-stay hotel in Kennesaw.

My mother had kept up with the payments so I would have a familiar place to return to when I was released, which I greatly appreciated. My parents wanted to give me the best chance for a fresh start. I had other ideas. I wanted to go back to being the old Lex.

But for the first time, I didn't have a plan. I was unsure of myself, not certain what direction to take. I jumped right back into the old routine—light buzz in the morning, pre-workout lunch, workout, then a hard buzz at night.

■ ■ ■

A few weeks later as I was leaving the gym, I heard a familiar voice call out my name.

"Hey, Lex!"

I turned around, and there he was—the jail chaplain! I had already forgotten his name. I was shocked to see him. *How did he find me? There must be hundreds of gyms in Atlanta's northern suburbs.*

"Steve Baskin," he said, smiling and holding out his hand. "I'm ready to get back in shape if you're willing to help."

I was initially caught off guard but quickly recovered. *This might be fun. I'll work him so hard and make him so sore, he'll never set foot in a gym again.* "Why don't you pick me up at my hotel at eleven o'clock tomorrow morning?" I said.

"That would be great," he said. "I'll see you then."

■ ■ ■

When Pastor Steve knocked at my hotel door the next morning, I didn't answer. I was sure that if I waited long enough without coming out, he'd just give up and call it a day. A half hour later, I peeked out of my window. He was still there, patiently sitting in his car in the parking lot. I could tell he wasn't going anywhere.

This guy just doesn't get it. I figured I had no choice other than to come out, go to the gym, and run him through a Matsuda-style workout, in hopes that he'd leave me alone from now on.

At the gym, I gave it to him with both barrels, but he never complained once. By the end of the workout, I could tell he was totally exhausted.

When he dropped me off at the hotel, he said, "What time should I be here tomorrow?"

I couldn't believe my ears. However, I knew that when he woke up in the morning, he'd be so sore he would probably have trouble even getting out of bed. But the next morning, there he was, sitting in the parking lot, ready to go to the gym. In spite of my greatest efforts to make him quit, he was there every morning. I soon realized he was in it for the long haul. He began losing weight and adding muscle and was elated with the results. Surprisingly, I began to enjoy training him and watching his progress.

Soon, we weren't just going to the gym together. Pastor Steve volunteered to help me take care of issues I needed to address. First, he went with me to help smooth things over with my probation officer. Then he accompanied me to the Cobb County Courthouse to pay some additional fines I thought I owed. Instead of having to pay, they refunded me $700 that had been overpaid! I couldn't believe it. I began calling Pastor Steve "my lucky charm."

"You know, Lex, I think we should go down to the DMV and try to get your driver's license back," he said one day.

I was under the impression that it would be a long time before I would ever get my driver's license back.

"No harm in trying," Pastor Steve said.

Whatever, Pastor Steve. But we walked into the DMV and *boom!* I walked out with a new driver's license with no hassles or delays.

After one workout, Pastor Steve invited me out to lunch. On our way there, he said he needed to make a quick stop at Walmart.

"Do you want to come in with me?" he asked.

"Steve, I've never been in a Walmart in my life. I've always been a Saks Fifth Avenue/Whole Foods kind of guy."

"Well, come check it out," he said.

As we walked around the store, we were constantly greeted by wrestling fans and well-wishers. "Hey, Lex, great to see you out and about!"

We then went to the Golden Corral for lunch, another place I had never been before. It was a gigantic buffet extraordinaire; I loved it! Once again, people came up to me to say hello. I realized this was all part of Pastor Steve's plan, to get me out to places that regular folks—my wrestling fans—frequented, places where everyone was glad to see me. Truthfully, after all the bad stuff that had happened, their reactions initially caught me off guard. I didn't know what to make of it. But to be honest, it felt kind of good.

I was getting more and more comfortable hanging out with Pastor Steve, and eventually, I started asking him questions about religion. "So what's the difference between Catholics and Protestants?" "Why are there so many different denominations?" "Why do bad things happen to good people?" "How do you explain dinosaurs?" I peppered him with all types of questions. He always answered thoughtfully or admitted when he didn't have all the answers. I appreciated his honesty.

■ ■ ■

One day I was out running errands with Pastor Steve and decided to stay in the car and wait for him to finish. I noticed a religious leaflet in the side-door pocket with the words *God's Simple Plan of Salvation* in bold print. I began reading it, but when I saw Pastor Steve coming back to the car, I stuck it in my pocket. I didn't mention anything to him.

That evening, I took the leaflet out and read through it. I understood the words but not what the words meant. Phrases like "being born again" made no sense to me. I had already been born. *How could I be born again?* I mulled it over. It didn't seem very simple to me. For the next couple of weeks, I read and reread that small leaflet, but I never asked Pastor Steve about it.

Not long after, Pastor Steve asked, "Do you remember Dr. Frady, the head chaplain at the Cobb County Jail?"

The name didn't ring a bell with me.

"He pastors Clarkdale First Baptist Church. I often attend the evening services there. It's casual. You don't have to dress up. Would you like to meet me there this Sunday evening? We can grab some grub afterward."

It was the question that I had been waiting for, wondering when he was going to ask it.

"Sure," I said, thinking at least we'd get good food.

"The service starts at seven o'clock. I'll meet you there."

21
RECONSTRUCTION ON THE ROCK

I arrived at the church at 7:10 p.m. I didn't see Steve's car in the parking lot, but I figured he might have gotten a ride with someone else. Now that I was there, I was nervous. I walked up to the large white doors and put my hand on one of the gold handles, but I hesitated. I had a major case of cold feet. I turned around, went back to my car, and sat there for another ten minutes debating with myself. *I'm really late. I should just go home and call Steve later.* But if Steve was waiting inside, I didn't want to let him down.

I went to the front door for the second time and hesitated again, almost bailing. Instead, I slipped inside and quietly found a seat in the last pew. Up front, behind the pulpit, Dr. Frady was into his message. I heard him mention that his text was from the Sermon on the Mount, when Jesus was speaking to a large group of people. And then he read Jesus' words:

Whosoever heareth these sayings of mine, and doeth them,
I will liken him unto a wise man, which built his house
upon a rock: and the rain descended, and the floods came,
and the winds blew, and beat upon that house; and it fell
not: for it was founded upon a rock. And every one that
heareth these sayings of mine, and doeth them not, shall be
likened unto a foolish man, which built his house upon the
sand: and the rain descended, and the floods came, and the
winds blew, and beat upon that house; and it fell: and great
was the fall of it. (Matthew 7:24-27, KJV)

"When we build our lives around other people, money, or what
we consider success," Dr. Frady said, "we're putting our faith in trinkets and baubles that will not last, things that we ultimately can't
count on. What's your life based upon? The rock or the sand? When
your life is based upon the Rock, your house will stand strong, no
matter what."

He's describing my life. My life has been built completely on the sand.

I envisioned the Sugarloaf mansion, all my cars, clothes, and jewelry, all my "trinkets and baubles" I had accumulated—everything
that I had considered the evidence of my success—piled together
on a sandy beach. Suddenly I saw a huge wave crashing onshore,
and within moments, everything was gone, washed out to sea. It all
seemed so real.

The impact of what Dr. Frady said nearly took my breath away.
It seemed like he was standing just a foot away from me as he spoke,
and I pressed back into the pew as far as I could, trying to put space
between the two of us. Of course, in reality, Dr. Frady was still up
front, and there were many rows of pews between us. Still, I was
unaware of any other people in the church; I felt like it was just him
and me alone in the room. Even though Dr. Frady's lips were moving, I truly believed it was God—not him—speaking directly to me.

Everything I had believed to be so important—chasing fortune and glory—was empty, without substance.

Dr. Frady asked if anyone wanted to commit their lives to Jesus Christ and invited them to come to the front of the church. I conveniently took the opportunity to head the other way—out the door and to my car.

I was sweating, and my heart was racing. I didn't know what was going on with me. *Oh, man, that was a close call,* I thought to myself.

I called Steve later that night. "I didn't see you at church."

"I'm sorry," Steve said. "I couldn't make it. I left a message on your phone."

"Oh." I had a bad habit of not checking my voice mail messages.

"By the way, did you tell Dr. Frady I was going to be there tonight?"

"No, I didn't."

I was convinced that I had been set up, that Pastor Steve had tipped off Dr. Frady so that he specifically chose the theme of his message to target me.

I couldn't stop thinking about Dr. Frady's message the entire week, the contrast of the rock and the sand. All of my bad decisions and what I had based those decisions upon—the things that I believed had made me successful to myself and other people—really had been a sham. It was all built on the sand.

I kept pulling out the little pamphlet I'd found in Steve's car and reading it, but it still didn't quite connect with me.

■ ■ ■

It was April 23, 2006, and Steve and I were hanging out at my hotel watching a Los Angeles Lakers game on television. We were casually sitting and talking when I decided to bring up what had been dogging me all week. I reached under my bodybuilding magazines on the coffee table and pulled out the pamphlet.

"I got this from your car," I said, "and I've been going over it a bunch of times. I just don't get it."

Steve immediately jumped to his feet. I had never seen him move so quickly, with such urgency.

For some reason, I was pulled to my feet too.

"What are we standing here for?" I asked.

"This is the moment I've been waiting for," Steve replied.

"What do you mean by that?"

"Lex, be totally honest. Are you truly happy with the direction your life's taking right now?"

"No," I admitted. "Honestly, I've made a complete mess of things."

"Lex, that's okay. We all make a mess of things when we try to do things on our own. But there's a much better way for all of us. God has always had a plan for each one of our lives, including yours."

"Steve, I've done so much stuff. It's too late for me." I thought I had gone too far down the road and didn't think I could ever make up for what I had done. It was the most honest I had ever been with myself.

"We all fall short when we do it all on our own."

I knew Steve was right. I was weary. After trying to do things myself, I had only managed to make a wreck out of my life. I had been a rudderless ship, beyond hope.

"You don't have to fight anymore," Steve said. "Move over and let God take control. Let Him steer."

Yes, I was ready to surrender, ready for somebody else to take charge of my life. I wanted to get out of the way; I wanted to be saved from myself. It was never clear to me until that moment.

"What do I need to do?"

"Ask God for His forgiveness."

"Man, all that stuff I've done and the people I've hurt—I can be forgiven for everything right now?"

"Yes, you can."

Steve got down on his knees in front of the couch, and I followed suit.

I repeated the words that Steve prayed. "God, I'm a sinner." With those first words, I broke down. "Jesus, please forgive me. Come into my heart and take over my life."

And then an incredible thing happened. The same brilliant light that I had seen in my dream—that tiny speck that had pulled me out of the muck and darkness—I felt it inside of me. It purged me from the inside out with such power that I thought I was going to spontaneously combust! It was like being power-washed by light, scoured clean of the darkness inside of me; I had never felt anything like it before.

As I stood up, it dawned on me: I had been kneeling over the very same spot on the couch where I had overdosed nearly ten months earlier. Only God could have orchestrated that—for me to be raised to new life with Him in the exact place where I had nearly died. There was no doubt in my mind that something supernatural had just happened.

22

A WHOLE NEW LIFE

I was immediately aware that I was embarking on a brand-new journey. I felt completely different from the inside out. I realized I wasn't alone anymore. I sensed God was going to guide me from now on, which gave me incredible peace and relief. Instead of isolating myself, I became more outgoing and was excited to be around people again.

When I asked Steve what was happening to me, he said it was the Holy Spirit living inside of me and working through me. I wasn't sure what that meant, but it sure felt good!

Everything in life became fascinating to me, and I wanted to take it all in. I was like a kid in a candy store.

I started bugging Steve. "What's next? Do I go to church with you every Sunday? What should I do?" Suddenly, I was hungry to learn new things instead of being a know-it-all. That was a big change for me.

"Lex, it's a great idea to go to church regularly. But even before that happens, I want you to read the Bible, because God will speak into your life through it. It is holy and inspired, the living Word of God."

Steve brought me a brand-new black leather Bible with the words *Holy Bible* in gold letters on the front. He had written my name on the inside. He added his signature and dated it so neither of us would forget when I had accepted Jesus into my life in that hotel room. Even though I had owned many expensive things in my life, this Bible meant more to me than all of them put together. I was very touched. I marveled at this precious gift, the second Bible Steve had given me. This one would never be carelessly tossed on the floor like the first one had been.

"Where do I start reading?" I asked Steve.

"Start with one of the Gospels."

"What are those?" I asked.

"Gospel means 'good news.' In the Bible, a Gospel is a book that tells about Jesus' life on earth. There are four Gospels in the Bible—Matthew, Mark, Luke, and John. Many people recommend you begin with John, but I prefer Matthew, myself."

I started with the book of Matthew, along with an easy-to-follow study guide that Steve gave me to help me understand it better. I found it all so exciting, especially when I came to the verses in Matthew 7 that Dr. Frady had quoted. I read them over and over again. These were the words of truth that had convicted me at the back of Dr. Frady's church.

When I began bugging Steve about going to church, he first wanted to explain why we went to church. "It's a place to praise and worship God through hymns and songs that will often speak to your heart. It's a chance to gather together and hear God's message. You'll also find that we encourage each other with our stories. Over time, you'll begin to recognize the gifts that you can give to others in the church and the community to make a difference in people's lives."

One day I said to Steve, "I sure wish I could pray like you. I feel awkward when I try to do it. How do I learn to pray like you?"

"Don't worry about learning how to pray. The Holy Spirit will guide you over time. The key question is *why* we pray—it's to praise God for what He is doing in our lives and to give thanks to Him. And it's also intercession."

"What is that?"

"Praying for other people's needs. We can ask God for things in prayer. He already knows everything we need and want, but He wants us to come to Him anyway. When you pray, He'll give you divine guidance."

It was time to make another change.

"Lex, have you ever thought of moving out of this place?" Steve asked, looking around my hotel room. "If I had an extra room, would you consider moving in with me for a while?"

I thought it was one of the best offers I had heard in a long time. It was a whole new life for me, like a breath of fresh air.

■ ■ ■

My friendship with Sting had instantly taken on a new meaning. I understood everything that had taken place in his life because now I was experiencing it myself. We were like two brothers being reunited. He asked me to appear with him along with Nikita Koloff on *Praise the Lord*, airing on the Trinity Broadcasting Network. It was incredible for the three of us to be together, hanging out at Steve's house in California. Nikita and I had been adversaries in the ring, but now we were spiritual brothers.

Everything was happening so quickly. Even though I was reunited with old friends and was spending time with a new family of believers, I would often get extremely emotional thinking about what I had done in the past. It would come in waves and would bring me to tears. I had such regret for what I had put my entire family through. It was a deep pain and heaviness I carried in my heart. For the first time, I was feeling godly remorse. But I didn't know what to do about it.

On Memorial Day weekend I was invited to a holiday picnic at Dr. Frady's house that turned out to be a surprise birthday party for me. Halfway through the party, Dr. Frady's wife, Jan, pulled me aside and said that her husband wanted to see me in his study.

My mind momentarily flashed back to the times I had been summoned to the principal's office at school. *Did I do something wrong already?*

I cautiously entered his study. When Dr. Frady asked me to have a seat in his chair, I knew he had something serious to say to me.

"I don't know all the details of your life," he said, "but I've read the headlines. I know a lot of bad stuff has happened. But there is one thing you need to understand, Lex. God has forgiven you for all that. That also means you have to be able to forgive yourself. Otherwise, you'll be totally useless to the Kingdom. You've got to be able to move forward with your life. What's happened in the past is like a bell that has been rung, and you can't unring it. Carrying around things from the past will only weigh you down. You have to let it go. If you keep holding on to unforgiveness for yourself and others, it will become a cancer; it will fester and grow inside of you.

"But you don't have to have that cancer inside of you; God has given you a clean slate. You've got to get out there and share your story with others. God commands us to do that, to share the good news of the gospel.

"That doesn't mean there aren't consequences for your past. You can apologize; some people may accept your apology, and some may not. That's just the way it is."

He encouraged me to continue spending time with godly people, to read the Bible, and to share my story as much as possible. As I left, I was thankful that God had brought people like the Fradys and Steve Baskin into my life at just the right time.

■ ■ ■

In June, Sting invited me to take part in an Athletes in Action conference in Phoenix. It was encouraging for me to interact with so many other athletes who were putting God first in their lives. That same weekend, Sting and I were scheduled to appear at a high-security youth detention center, along with some of the other Christian athletes.

It was certainly déjà vu for me to walk in there. We met beforehand with the person who had arranged everything and talked about the order of events. One of the other athletes said to me, "How about you, Lex? Would you like to give your testimony?"

"Testimony? What is that?" The only testimony I was aware of took place in a courtroom.

"It's just telling your story."

"No way," I said, "you guys have got this covered."

Sting was an old hand at this. After he shared how God had changed his life, I suddenly asked him if I could have the microphone for a moment. Sting looked surprised.

"The only reason I am here today is because I received permission from my probation officer to come. I'm a convicted felon." That got the audience's attention.

You could have heard a pin drop in the room. All eyes were on me. I understood exactly where they were, because I had been there. I began to share from my heart. The Holy Spirit took over. "My pursuit of what seemed cool brought only emptiness into my life. But God gave me a second chance. He can give you a second chance as well. What do you want to stand on—the sand or the rock? You've been lied to and let down by people all your lives. Jesus won't let you down, no matter what." I had given my very first testimony.

God broke down many young men's hearts that day, and it was a humbling experience to be part of it. And then to cap things off, I was part of a big baptism party at the hotel. Sting baptized me in the swimming pool that night, a very special moment for both of us.

The next morning, I went with Sting and a group of athletes to Phoenix First Assembly of God, the megachurch pastored by Tommy

Barnett. We were introduced onstage as a group and waved at the congregation. As I was exiting offstage, the man holding the microphone snagged me and announced to the crowd that I had just been saved. Everyone cheered. Then he said, "Lex, why don't you give us your testimony?" I was horrified, frozen in fear. If I could have disappeared right then, I would have. I had certainly been in front of large crowds before in my life, but not in this kind of situation. I wondered how long I needed to talk. I spotted Pastor Tommy in the front row, flashing his fingers at me, giving me instructions. Borrowing from my wrestling days, I did a five-minute promo for Jesus. Then Tommy Barnett ran up onstage and gave me a big hug. I had just given testimony number two.

It turned out to be two power-packed months for me. No matter what I did from that point on, I had to share my story with others.

■ ■ ■

Dr. Frady and Steve Baskin are dedicated men of faith who serve and follow Jesus. Living with Steve gave me the opportunity to observe firsthand what that means. Every morning I watched Steve get up early for his devotional time. My first inclination was to give him space and go to the gym for a workout.

But it wasn't long before I was right there beside him. He really rubbed off on me. A first-thing-in-the-morning devotional became second nature to me. What had once been my bedtime sleep-it-off hour during my wrestling days had now become my wake-up-with-God hour—another prime example of the 180-degree changes that were happening in my life.

My Christian family was growing too. I was around people of faith all the time, and I was having a blast—going out to eat, exploring new local places like Stone Mountain, doing ordinary things with my new friends, and laughing the whole time. There was another dramatic change: before I realized it, I began doing things for other people! It was exciting and enjoyable to give without expecting anything in return.

I followed Dr. Frady's advice to capitalize on what I was passionate about and began writing about fitness and nutrition for a magazine called *Christian Living*. I wanted to reach regular folks, not just elite athletes, with the message of a healthy lifestyle. God broadened my perspective about the master plan I had always had. Making a profit wasn't my driving force anymore. I just wanted to help people.

I was definitely headed in a new direction with Jesus at my side.

23
BECOMING
A NEW CREATION

Everything about me was changing, even more than I realized. People who knew me from the past would say, "Lex, you're really different. You're being nice now. Your body language, your mannerisms, your facial expressions—nothing's the same."

Around this time, I was interviewed on a popular local radio sports show that I had been on many times before. At the first break, the show's host—who had known me for years—stepped out of the studio. "Who is that guy in there?" he said half-seriously to the friend who had come with me. "Is that really Lex?" He couldn't believe how different I was.

At the gym, I began going around and helping the younger guys, giving them tips and encouragement. Before, I had always made it clear by my body language that I wanted to be left alone. Now the other guys began to flock to me to get on the Lex plan—following my workout routine. A lot of them asked me how much it cost. "It doesn't cost anything," I said, "but there's one condition. You need to find other guys in the gym who you can teach the plan to." That put big smiles on their faces. As the weeks passed, just like Pastor Steve, they began getting great results.

I found that I was really enjoying coaching others. It was also a great opportunity to let these guys know that with proper training and nutrition, they could become as big and strong as they wanted to be, without resorting to PEDs. Great results spoke much louder than a lecture about staying off drugs. Yes, they were impressed with my physique, but I'd joke with them, saying, "If I can do this at my age without steroids and drugs, just think what you can do at your age." After a great workout, we'd all go to the Golden Corral buffet. I used it as a training table to instruct the young men on how to eat properly. It was also a chance to hang out and have fun with each other.

The regulars at the gym certainly noticed a change in me too, especially my vocabulary. "Hey, Lex," they'd say, "you don't swear anymore." At first I thought, *Yeah, I do,* and then I realized, *Well, I guess I don't.*

When guys would ask, "Hey, Lex, who's that woman I saw you with?" and I'd say, "She's a friend," they'd snicker at my comment. To be honest, for the first time in my life, I could enjoy the company of a woman without thinking we were going to end up in bed together. It was a great feeling to have that pressure gone.

When Steve and I would go out to grab a steak, I could relax at the bar, sipping on ice water, instead of having cocktails and popping pills. So many of the things that had once consumed me, I didn't care about anymore. This lifestyle change wasn't something I had been doing consciously; it was just who I was becoming.

As great as everything was going, I was really struggling with the pain in my hip. It was becoming constant and agonizing. I thought going to the chiropractor, getting massages, and doing long stretches after my workouts would remedy the situation, but it was only getting worse. Taking a couple of Advil and putting ice on my hip wasn't doing the trick either. I was beginning to realize that sooner rather than later, I needed to see an orthopedic doctor.

■ ■ ■

My nephew, Greg, came to visit me in the spring of 2007. Greg is a personal trainer, so I wasn't surprised when he wanted to stop by a local bodybuilding show. We ended up sitting with a female pro bodybuilder named Liza, whom I knew from the Gold's Gym I went to. As we talked, I learned that Liza was a physician's assistant. A few days after the show, one of my friends asked if he could give my contact information to Liza. "Sure," I said, not thinking much of it.

When Liza called me, she got right to the point. "At the show I noticed how you were really favoring that right hip. I want you to get that checked out. If it's okay with you, I want to make an appointment for you with a friend of mine, Dr. Terrell, at Pinnacle Orthopaedics."

I really appreciated her concern. I was feeling pretty gimpy by that point, trying more and more not to be seen limping around. I was in so much pain that I realized I shouldn't put it off any longer. I would get Dr. Terrell's professional opinion, even though I still thought my problem was with my L5 vertebra and I'd be able to work it out.

When I arrived at his office, I had X-rays done, then waited for his assessment. When Dr. Terrell came into the examination room with his assistant, he put up two sets of X-rays and illuminated them—one was of my hips, and the other was of a normal pair of hips. He didn't say anything for a minute. Then he asked, "How on earth were you able to walk from your car upstairs to this office?"

His question caught me off guard. "I don't know. I just did. Why are you asking me that?"

Dr. Terrell showed me the difference between my hips and the healthy set of hips. "Here's a normal set of hips. Yours don't look like that. If you want any quality of life, if you just want to be able to get around, you need to get both hips replaced. Take a look at your left hip. It definitely needs to be done. But that's not the first priority. You don't even have a right hip anymore. Your femur is resting on your pelvic bone because your right hip has basically emulsified itself; it is completely gone. There aren't any other options. We'll do the right one first, then we can do the left hip a year later."

He paused. "I can't imagine the constant pain you must be in. You'll feel 100 percent better immediately afterward."

Now it was my turn to be silent. *My body is breaking down. I'm not the invincible Cyborg.* It was a harsh reality to face. This news meant two major surgeries with almost two years of downtime—not exactly what I had in mind for my fitness and nutrition game plan.

My response took Dr. Terrell by surprise. "To minimize the downtime, can you do both hips at once?"

"To be honest with you, Lex, I don't know. We've never done bilateral hip replacement surgery before. But I'll check with our hip specialist, Dr. Swayze, and get back to you."

After extensive consultation, I finally got the good news—they were giving it the green light. These were my kind of guys!

■ ■ ■

The seven-hour surgery was scheduled for the second week of November at WellStar Kennestone Hospital in Marietta, Georgia. Things were progressing nicely into the fall. I was working hard on a new company called "Total Package Fitness" that I was putting together for a January launch.

I had gotten an invitation to an autograph show in San Francisco for late October, which I accepted. It would be my last out-of-town trip for a while.

Going into my surgery, I wanted to be in the best shape of my life, especially my upper body. I knew I would have to back off a little bit when I was in rehab. So while I could, I pushed myself with heavy, intense two-a-day workouts.

I'd begun to feel a slight, intermittent burning sensation between my shoulder blades after my workouts. But I wasn't worried. I figured it was just a pinched nerve my chiropractor could work on. *No pain, no gain.*

24
THE CHALLENGE

I was booked on a red-eye flight to San Francisco for the autograph show, so I had the entire day to get things ready. I was glad that I could get in one more early-evening workout at the gym before I left. There would be time for me to come home, shower, grab my bag, and then head to the airport.

My bilateral hip surgery was ten days away. A number of my friends and family wanted me to cancel the trip, stay at home, and rest. I assured them this was going to be quick—I'd fly out, do the show, catch a red-eye back, and meet my friends on Saturday for our favorite breakfast buffet at the Golden Corral. It was going to be easy. I would be in San Francisco for less than twenty-four hours.

Everything was going smoothly. I got my errands done, then had an intense shoulders/traps/neck workout. When I got on the plane, my body was still settling down. My muscles were pumped, but that was normal after such a heavy workout. I was ready to kick back and relax.

Once I settled into my aisle seat, I began conversing with the young woman to my left in the window seat. There was an empty seat between us. She had just graduated from the University of Georgia and was heading to California for her first job. I could tell she was very excited. Not wanting to dampen her enthusiasm, I let her tell me all about it. The conversation that I thought would be a couple of minutes long turned into a couple of hours.

Finally, as I attempted to face forward and lean back in my seat, I felt an intense burning sensation down my neck and between my shoulder blades. It took a couple of minutes to subside. But I figured it was just a kink in my neck from my head being turned to the left for so long.

I arrived at my hotel around 2 a.m. By the time I checked in and got to my room, I was ready to crash. I was exhausted. I thought I'd catch a few hours of sleep, get up for my devotional time, have breakfast, and then head to the Cow Palace for the autograph session.

I looked at the clock. It was about 3 a.m. Because of my hip pain, the best way for me to sleep was on my left side with a pillow between my legs. I grabbed a pillow, but when I tried to lift my right leg up, it was like lead. It wouldn't move. I had to physically lift my leg with my hands. *That's weird*, I thought. But I was so tired that I just closed my eyes and fell asleep.

Suddenly, I was jolted awake by the same unbelievable pain between my shoulder blades that I had felt on the airplane. This time something was different. I couldn't move anything except my head and shoulders. Terrified, I tried to rock myself over to the edge of the bed so I could reach the telephone on the nightstand and call for help. Instead, I fell to the floor, doubled over. My chin was pressed into my chest, making it nearly impossible to breathe.

I cried out, but my voice was faint and raspy. I could barely breathe, let alone speak. Feeling absolutely helpless, I began to panic. *If someone doesn't find me, I'm going to die.*

Right then, I felt the presence of God envelop the room. The pain instantly subsided. I became calm, my breathing became regular, and I knew everything was going to be okay. I was not alone. It was supernatural.

I wasn't sure how much time had passed before there was a knock at the door and I heard the sound of a piece of paper being slipped under it. A thought flashed through my mind: *If someone is still standing at the door, that person might be able to hear me.*

I forced my words out. "Help! Who's there? I need help!"

"Is that you, Lex?" Miraculously, the person had heard me!

"Yeah, I need help!"

"Well, open the door."

"I can't."

The man in the hallway was involved with the Malice in the Palace fanfest that weekend. He had been distributing the itinerary to the participants' rooms. Fortunately for me, he had once been a first responder, so he acted quickly.

As I had been lying there, I realized I hadn't hydrated myself much after my workout. *Maybe that's why my entire body has shut down.* So as soon as the paramedics broke into my room (I had fastened the dead bolt), I said calmly, "Do you have any Gatorade and bananas? I think if I get something to drink and get some potassium in me, I'll be fine."

They gave me a funny look. "No, Lex, you need to go to the hospital right now."

In the ambulance, the paramedics admitted they were huge wrestling fans. "Don't worry, Lex. You're going to be all right. We'll get you to the best place possible." They began bouncing hospital names off each other, finally agreeing that Stanford Hospital, forty miles away, was where we needed to go. I don't know whether or not they were overstepping their bounds in making that decision, but either way, I was along for the ride.

■ ■ ■

In the hospital's emergency room, a male nurse asked, "Lex, when was the last time you went to the bathroom?"

"Last night," I said.

"In that case, we're going to have to catheterize you."

That concerned me. As much as I was attempting to remain positive, I began to realize that I wasn't going to walk right out of the hospital this time.

I still had no idea what had happened to me, and no one was able to give me information. They were running a battery of tests and had to wait for the results.

Finally, on Sunday, the entire neurology team came to my room to talk to me. "From what we can determine so far, you've injured your spinal cord. There is a lot of swelling from your C5 vertebra down to the T5 vertebra. We have to do a lot more testing, but for now we'll give you an anti-inflammatory to help alleviate the swelling."

I couldn't believe it. *How in the world did I do that?*

From the looks on their faces, I could tell this was a real serious deal.

Before I had time to dwell on it, I received a phone call from Sting—the first person to track me down. It was comforting to hear his voice.

"What happened?"

"I did something to my spinal cord, but they're still doing tests."

"I can fly out there right away," Sting said.

"I appreciate that, but there's nothing you can do at this point. I'm where I need to be, surrounded by great medical staff." It was truly a blessing to be at Stanford. They ran every test known to man; they were professional and thorough. With the information I had given them and the results of the tests, they hypothesized what had probably happened: the combination of my heavy workout before my flight and sitting on the plane with my head awkwardly turned had set my neck up for the "perfect storm." I had cut off the blood flow to my central spinal cord, which caused bruising and massive swelling. We'll never know how long the blood flow was cut off. Once that occurs, the damage to the spinal cord is done. It doesn't matter how it happens. The result is the same: paralysis.

On Monday, Pastor Steve arrived to spend a few days with me. I could sense that my family was panicking. But I could feel God telling me to be upbeat and positive and to reassure them that everything was going to be okay.

Over the next ten days, other friends flew out to California to be with me. My doctors told me that we would have to wait for the swelling to recede. It was unclear how much function I would ever regain—if any. The Stanford medical staff told me that I would need to begin physical therapy immediately. The neurology team said that there were only a few facilities in the country that they would recommend, other than Stanford.

"There's a place in Denver and then another place called the Shepherd Center," the doctor said.

"The Shepherd Center. Where's that?"

"Atlanta, Georgia."

"That's where I live!"

"The Shepherd Center would be our first choice, but it's difficult to get into; there is always a long waiting list."

I knew it would be better to be closer to my family and friends. The Shepherd Center told me there were no rooms available, but I would be put on a waiting list. The following day a room miraculously opened up, but they could hold it for only forty-eight hours. We couldn't arrange for a medevac that quickly, so I flew on a commercial Delta flight with a nurse and a friend. We took up two rows. I was strapped in, but my traveling companions had to hold me up the entire flight because my body kept sliding down in the seat.

When we arrived in Atlanta, an ambulance was waiting on the tarmac at the bottom of the stairs that were rolled next to the plane. I was getting door-to-door service. The owner of the ambulance company, who was a huge wrestling fan, had pulled some strings. She called to make sure everything was being taken care of. I smiled when she introduced herself. Her name was Faith.

25
THE SHEPHERD CENTER

We arrived at the Shepherd Center around 6 a.m. to be admitted. I couldn't see much from my position lying on the gurney as I was rolled through the entrance, into an elevator, and then down the hall to my room. Everything was happening fast. But I did catch my room number when we made the turn. Room 316! *Unbelievable.* John 3:16 is probably the most quoted verse in the Bible.

Inside the room, two nurses were waiting for me. I read their name tags: Comfort and Grace. Right then I knew that I was in the right place and realized once again that God was totally in charge of my situation.

My sister, Barb, came in a few minutes later. It was definitely good to be back in Atlanta.

In the next few hours, I was introduced to my entire medical team, led by Dr. Bilsky. Everyone was so positive and caring.

During one of my first days in therapy, someone said, "There's Mr. Shepherd."

"There's a Mr. Shepherd?" I thought it was just the name of the facility. In 1973, twenty-two-year-old James Shepherd, a recent graduate from the University of Georgia, suffered a spinal cord injury while bodysurfing. He was paralyzed from the neck down. After a five-week hospital stay, he was flown to the Denver rehab facility that I had first heard about when I was at Stanford. The Shepherd family wanted to establish a similar facility in the Southeast, and in 1975 they opened a six-bed unit in leased space in an Atlanta hospital. As the need grew, so did the Shepherd Center. It is now one of the premiere medical, research, and rehabilitation facilities for people with spinal cord and brain injuries.

Within approximately a week, my Shepherd team was ready to meet with me, Barb, and Pastor Steve.

They laid out their plan. "Lex, our goal is to prepare you to become as self-sufficient as possible. You are a C5-C6 quadriplegic. There's always hope; however, realistically, there is very little chance of you regaining any significant movement whatsoever from the neck down.

"We'll be fitting you for a power wheelchair. We'll be checking out where you live to determine whether ramps are necessary, to see how the bathroom is set up and if you will be able to get in and out of a shower, etc. Once home, you will need round-the-clock care."

"For how long will I need that?"

"Permanently."

From the moment it happened, I'd had a sense of foreboding that this was a very serious injury—more than something that could be repaired with surgery. My fear was now confirmed.

From the looks on Barb's and Pastor Steve's faces, I could see how devastating this all sounded to them. But God continued to give me a real peace about the entire situation. I had a lot of confidence in the staff and the facility I was in, so I told them, "It's all going to be okay."

■ ■ ■

I incorporated my devotional time into my new routine at the Shepherd Center. Early in the morning, the nursing tech on duty would prop me up in bed, open my Bible, and lay it on top of a pillow placed across me so I could see it. I spent most mornings meditating on Proverbs 3:5-6, which I had highlighted in yellow prior to my injury. The words in these two verses had been going through my mind over and over again ever since I had been lying on the hotel room floor in San Francisco. "Trust in the LORD with all thine heart; and lean not unto thine own understanding. In all thy ways acknowledge him, and he shall direct thy paths" (KJV).

One particular morning, a couple of weeks after I had arrived at the Shepherd Center, during my devotions I became completely overwhelmed with emotion and began to weep uncontrollably. Up until this point, I'd been able to hold it together with God's help. I began to cry out to Him. *How could You let this happen to me? What am I going to do? What good am I now? I can't do anything for myself—I can't feed myself, I can't bathe myself, I can't even go to the bathroom on my own.* I felt like a totally useless blob of flesh lying there on that bed. How could I spend the rest of my life like this? *I thought You wanted me to go out there and share my story. What kind of story do I have now? Some warrior for Christ I've turned out to be!*

I was angry at God. Darkness and self-pity were gaining a foothold.

But as He often does, God responded to me through a friend's wise counsel. Ken, the hospital chaplain I had met the day I arrived, visited me regularly. We had become good friends. He noticed that I wasn't being my usual upbeat self and knew something was wrong. Instead of pitying me, he actually called me out on it.

"Lex, about 80 to 85 percent of the spinal cord injury patients here are young men who have grown up watching you on television. They idolize you. They are observing your every move in here, to see how you are handling all of this. They are playing off you in that physical therapy room. You've been an inspiration to them by the way you've conducted yourself. 'If Lex can do it, we can do it.'"

Ken's words sunk in deeply.

Okay, God, I get it. It's not about me. There's a purpose and a plan for everything, even this. I can be used right here, right now, to encourage others.

From that point on, I was determined to be a bright light to everyone there—to be positive with the other patients and the staff. I had a renewed purpose. God wasn't making any promises to me about my recovery. He just wanted me to trust Him one day at a time—to embrace what did work, not what didn't. I began approaching every day with a spirit of thankfulness.

One day I turned to God's words to the apostle Paul in 2 Corinthians 12:9 in *The Daily Walk Bible*. Paul had been struggling with a longtime physical problem and had begun questioning his effectiveness. As many times as I had read it before, now it was like I was seeing this verse for the very first time. "My grace is all you need. My power works best in weakness."

I was incredibly moved. God was showing me how our greatest adversities in life are bridges rather than burdens. When we are broken and truly surrendered, we are more useful for God. No more self-reliance. Weakness allows us to turn it all over to Him.

■ ■ ■

I was beginning to make gradual progress, like a steady drip of water from a faucet. First, I was able to lift my left big toe, then my left index finger; and later my left leg, then my right leg. Everyone was very encouraged.

I received so much support from family and friends—stacks of cards, well-wishes, and a whole lot of prayer, as well as a constant stream of visitors. My dear friend Nikita Koloff would drive all the way from Charlotte, North Carolina, and back the same day to pray with me. Sting would fly in as well. My orthopedic doctor, Dr. Terrell, and Liza came on different nights just to sit with me. Dr. Terrell hadn't abandoned the possibility of bilateral hip surgery for me. "If you can put any weight on those legs, even with a walker, we can go ahead and do it. It couldn't hurt." I loved his optimism.

After three months, I was released from the Shepherd Center as an inpatient and began the day program with the help of Pastor Steve's sister, Vickie, who volunteered to be my caregiver for two months. I was very thankful for that.

When I was able to stand with a walker, Dr. Terrell and Dr. Swayze thought it was time for my hip surgery. "No one knows if you will walk someday, but let's do it anyway. If you walk, it will be taken care of." We went ahead and did the surgery.

I continued my rehab every day at the Shepherd Center for the remainder of 2008, leasing a condo across the street for easy access.

My rehab was progressing incredibly well. I was now able to do things that the doctors had believed would never again be possible. I had gone from needing a walker to using two walking sticks with cuffs around my arms, then just a cane, and finally being able to walk short distances unassisted. It was truly a miracle of God.

I relearned how to feed myself, bathe myself, brush my teeth, go to the bathroom, do my own laundry—all things most of us take for granted. I had a completely new outlook on life. I was so thankful. By God's grace, in a year's time, I was able to live on my own!

■ ■ ■

Psalm 118:24 says, "This is the day the LORD has made. We will rejoice and be glad in it." I have wholeheartedly embraced this verse since my spinal cord injury, and I would never want to start my day without it.

In 2009, I renewed my lease at the condo across from the Shepherd

Center for a second year. I started doing outpatient therapy from 6 a.m. to noon, Monday through Friday. I'd motor across the street in my power wheelchair before the sun came up, ready to go to work. After a shower back at the condo, I'd return to Shepherd for lunch in the cafeteria and visit with families and patients in the afternoons during the week and on weekends. It was a privilege to serve in this way, to give back to my Shepherd family.

As the months passed, I began to gain strength in my upper and lower body and had more flexibility. My endurance was improving, along with my ability to walk and stand on my feet for longer periods of time. I even began to navigate some stairs. Some of my biggest thrills may seem like the smallest of accomplishments—like opening up a soda can, unscrewing a lid off a jar, plugging in my cell phone, and eating with regular silverware.

My next big step was beginning to drive a car again. I felt like a sixteen-year-old getting my first driver's license, only this was more exciting! Once I got comfortable enough, I started driving around in a parking lot first, then down the block and around town. Soon I felt ready for my first big solo road trip—a four-hour drive to Charlotte, North Carolina, to visit my good friend Nikita Koloff.

We talked en route. "How close are you?" he asked me.

"I'm about an hour away."

"Who are you with?" he asked.

"Nobody."

"What do you mean, nobody?"

"I'm driving myself!"

"You've got to be kidding me!"

"No, I'm serious."

Nikita was as excited as I was. It was a great moment shared with a wonderful friend.

More and more, I was leaving the cocoon of Shepherd and venturing out into the real world again. It was time for the next big move. With my increased mobility and ability to drive, I wanted to find a more centralized location, still near the Shepherd Center but closer to my friends and family.

Pastor Steve and I went exploring and found the perfect spot about fifteen minutes away. This condo was located in a village setting with tons of restaurants, a barbershop—and a Starbucks, of course! I was looking forward to walking around my new neighborhood for exercise and hanging out at my favorite coffee shop.

Another big moment was walking into a regular gym for the first time since my injury. All my workouts since then had been at the Shepherd Center. Words can't describe how ecstatic I felt in those familiar surroundings. Going to the gym was something that I had done all my life and never thought I would be able to do again.

Obviously, my workouts are different now than they used to be; I'm not pumping the heavy iron anymore. However, just to be able to work out on the machines for my upper and lower body and then hit the cardio on the treadmill, elliptical machine, or stationary bike are things that I have found a brand-new appreciation for. I still love going to the gym!

When I was at Shepherd, I had asked the staff, "What's the best way to increase my walking speed and mobility?"

"Walk," they replied. I've really taken that advice to heart. I've incorporated as much walking into my daily activity as I can. I walk at my local Walmart, Target, and grocery stores. I'm out and about, movin' and a-groovin', and making friends at the same time.

■ ■ ■

As I recovered, I also became more confident to get out there and share my story again. There was so much more to tell.

I began speaking at schools, churches, business groups—anyplace I could encourage others.

Remember my master plan that I pursued for most of my life? I'm now following the Master's plan. Total Package Fitness allows me the opportunity to coach, mentor, and assist others to implement a happier, healthier lifestyle. I guess you could call me a wellness or lifestyle coach. We discuss fitness and nutrition, as well as how to maintain a positive outlook and surround yourself with positive people and influences. We address better time and stress management strategies and emphasize getting enough rest and sleep. I've discovered that when I talk with people about various ways to improve their lives, a level of trust develops. This is a great door-opener to discuss the spiritual aspects of their lives. It enables me to share my faith with them and explain its vital importance in my life. Mentally fit, physically fit, spiritually fit—the trifecta—the total package!

I love how God utilizes our past experiences for the greater good.

I continue to volunteer my time at the Shepherd Center, especially talking with young men and women and their families who are facing the same things I did. It is an honor and a privilege to help in any way I can.

I work with ministries and organizations that help people struggling with addictions. Once again, God is using something that had caused so much pain and darkness in my life for the benefit of others.

God has also given me the opportunity to reconnect with wrestling. I am working with a new nonprofit organization called World Wrestling Outreach (WWO). Our goal is to impact the wrestling industry and its fans in a positive way. We will be coaching, mentoring, and training new talent, as well as assisting current or retired wrestlers in any way possible.

The WWO will also use the sport of professional wrestling as a community and evangelistic outreach on weekends. We plan to go into the schools on Fridays with a message about making positive choices. Saturday evenings we will hold a family-friendly fund-raising wrestling event, with local businesses, schools, and churches participating. Everything will be capped off with Sunday morning services in local churches, where the gospel message will be shared.

I am very thankful for all these opportunities God has provided and look forward to where He will lead me in the future. My journey continues. Praise God, hallelujah!

EPILOGUE
THE GOOD NEWS

When I was on my knees with Pastor Steve in that hotel room in 2006, I finally realized that I needed to be saved from myself. I had tried to do everything my own way, and it definitely wasn't working. My life had become a train wreck.

I believed that I was the one who was in charge of my destiny. After all, I had my master plan. I thought I had my future all mapped out. I embarked on a relentless quest for money, fame, glamour, and achievements. But I was never satisfied. Enough was never enough. The more I had, the more I desired. I was on an empty and futile chase. I was living proof of the "successful" man that Jesus described—a man who had gained the whole world but, in the process, was losing his own soul.

I was reaping exactly what I was sowing, especially with my double life. I wandered along with no sense of accountability, going from one bad decision to another. A series of compromises was leading me down a path of destruction for myself and everyone around me.

And yet I still didn't get it. I had no concept of God and did not acknowledge Him as the Creator of everything, including me. I wasn't aware of anything except me, myself, and I. In every situation, I thought I had all the answers.

Selfishness and pride were my biggest obstacles.

I needed to surrender myself to God.

That's true for all of us. It's only when we get to the end of ourselves that God can begin to do His work. He knows us better than anyone does, inside and out, because He made us. Each one of us is a unique person wonderfully created by Him with our distinctive gifts, talents, and abilities. And in His infinite wisdom, He has a plan and a purpose, a divine calling for each of us that we can discover if we yield our lives to Him.

When Jesus was asked which was the most important commandment, He replied, "'You must love the LORD your God with all your heart, all your soul, and all your mind.' This is the first and greatest commandment. A second is equally important: 'Love your neighbor as yourself'" (Matthew 22:37-39). Wow. How incredibly simple: love and honor God, love and serve others!

But before Jesus ascended to heaven, He gave us one more commandment: "Go into all the world and preach the Good News to everyone" (Mark 16:15). It's called the Great Commission, and it's the *only* reason I wrote this book. I was once a lost person who needed to hear the gospel of Jesus Christ, the Good News. Pastor Steve shared it with me. It's my privilege to share it with you. My hope and prayer is that you will accept God's free gift of eternal life and let Him begin working in your life, as He is doing in mine.

I now embrace the journey God has me on. I echo the words of the apostle Paul: "I press on to reach the end of the race and receive the heavenly prize for which God, through Christ Jesus, is calling us" (Philippians 3:14).

Won't you please join me on this incredible journey?

AN INVITATION TO THE JOURNEY

Each one of us is on a journey—a journey that begins at a different time, in a different place, and under different circumstances. My story may seem dramatically different from yours, but in reality, we are all alike: we are born separated from God. We all have that in common. The most important decision we need to make in our lives is whether we want to continue to live that way.

If you have read my story and want to take the steps I did to become a follower of Christ, here's what you need to do:

1. *Acknowledge that God is the Creator.* He is the Architect who created everything, and He "rules over everything" (Psalm 103:19).
2. *Die to yourself and be reborn in Christ.* Jesus never pulled any punches about what is missing in our lives, no matter how rich or successful or religious we are. He clearly spelled it out to a highly educated man named Nicodemus: "You must be born again" (John 3:7).
3. *Face the truth that you are a sinner.* Romans 3:23 tells us that "everyone has sinned; we all fall short of God's glorious standard." God is holy and cannot look on sin. Our sins

prevent us from having a relationship with Him. You can see from my story that my sins started out small and seemingly innocent but escalated over time. Big or small, our sins keep us separated from God and poison our souls.

4. *Confess to God that you are a sinner.* Romans 6:23 says that "the wages of sin is death, but the free gift of God is eternal life through Christ Jesus our Lord." Here is the Good News for all of us: "God showed his great love for us by sending Christ to die for us while we were still sinners" (Romans 5:8). Christ took our sins upon Himself and nailed them to the cross.

5. *Believe that Jesus is the one and only way to restore your relationship with God.* As He said, "I am the way, the truth, and the life. No one can come to the Father except through me" (John 14:6). There's no other way that we can be reconciled to God except through Jesus.

That day in the hotel room, Pastor Steve had me read Romans 10:9 out loud: "If you confess with your mouth that Jesus is Lord and believe in your heart that God raised him from the dead, you will be saved." Then he had me recite Romans 10:13: "Everyone who calls on the name of the LORD will be saved." When I read those two verses, I wept.

In an instant, I knew that "anyone who belongs to Christ has become a new person. The old life is gone; a new life has begun!" (2 Corinthians 5:17).

It will be a life filled with redemption, forgiveness, and the gift of the Holy Spirit to guide you—a life filled with "love, joy, peace, patience, kindness, goodness, faithfulness, gentleness, and self-control" (Galatians 5:22-23).

This doesn't mean that there won't be trials or adversities along the way, but you will never face them alone again. God will be beside you. He will never forsake you. God taught me that at the Shepherd Center. Each time I felt I couldn't go on, He said, "My grace is all you need. My power works best in weakness" (2 Corinthians 12:9).

But that wasn't all He taught me. He let me know that what I was going through would be a way for me to serve others. "He comforts us in all our troubles so that we can comfort others. When they are troubled, we will be able to give them the same comfort God has given us" (2 Corinthians 1:4).

I am stronger and richer than I have ever been because of the decision I made on April 23, 2006, to give my life to Jesus Christ. From that moment, I began building my life upon the Rock.

What about you? Do you want to begin a new life? Why not take the first step right now? Surrender. Build your life on Jesus the Rock, not on the sand (see Matthew 7:24). That is my desire for you. If you make that decision, I promise you that your life will never be the same.

LEX LUGER

ACKNOWLEDGMENTS

First and foremost, I want to thank God. Without Him, I wouldn't have this story to tell.

In addition, special thanks go out to the following people:

- Bonne Steffen and the entire team at Tyndale House Publishers
- John D. Hollis
- All my family and friends whom I love so much—you know who you are
- And a special shout-out to Michael Anthony Mooney, aka "The Great Moodini"

LEX LUGER

■ ■ ■

I want to thank God for His blessings and guidance in helping us bring Lex's story to life.

My role in this inspirational project wouldn't have been possible without the unconditional love and support of my wife, Regina, and our precocious young son, Davis. The two of them have long been my own personal bedrock, allowing me to persevere through life's toughest challenges.

I'd also like to thank my brother-in-law, Howard Davis Jr., as well as my close friends Kevin Tydings, Stewart Verdery, Rich Gable, Steve Metzger, and Curtis Bunn, among others, whose precious time and kind words always provided me with inspiration. Many friends found it ironic that I would someday be involved in a book project with one of the professional wrestlers we had watched together during college weekends.

Big props also go out to Bonne Steffen, our talented editor at Tyndale House Publishers whose tireless efforts helped make this book possible. Thanks, Bonne, for teaching me so much.

I also wish to recognize Matt Lacey for his time, valued insights, and passion in helping Lex and me put this story together in the best way.

I'll never forget the first time I met Lex Luger for lunch at the Shepherd Center in early June 2008. I had been slated to write a story about him for the *Atlanta Journal-Constitution* and had been looking forward to meeting him in person because I had been an avid professional wrestling fan when I was younger. I envisioned an older version of The Total Package, the man whom I had seen on television with the larger-than-life persona and sculpted physique. This Lex Luger was not that guy, at least not physically, since he was in rehabilitation for a devastating spinal cord injury. He is a deeply spiritual man, one who displayed tremendous grace and humility when discussing his many transgressions during his life. He and I hit it off right away and came to know one another very well.

The story I wrote about Lex in the *AJC* generated overwhelming public response that easily surpassed any such buzz created by previous sports stories I had done. Two years later, Lex asked me to partner with him on this book project, and I couldn't have been prouder.

Lex's story had always resonated with me on a very personal level because of my own doubts and shortcomings, albeit on a lesser scale and minus the intense public scrutiny. His well-chronicled mistakes had played out for the rest of us to see. In Lex, I saw glimpses of myself and my friends, all of us to varying degrees drifting aimlessly in search of life's true meaning. The story of Lex's redemption and powerful transformation through the love of our Lord and Savior Jesus Christ is one we should all heed.

I am a better man because Lex shared his story with me. And for that, I will always be grateful.

JOHN D. HOLLIS

ABOUT THE AUTHORS

LEX LUGER is a three-time world heavyweight wrestling champion who has held nearly every championship and title obtainable in professional wrestling. Prior to becoming a professional wrestler, Lex played college and professional football for a number of years.

As a wrestler, some of Lex's career highlights include belonging to the legendary "Four Horsemen" group, slamming Yokozuna on the USS *Intrepid* to kick off the Lex Express tour, and being one of the headliners of *Nitro*, during which he was the first to defeat world champion Hulk Hogan on national television.

In 2006, Lex experienced a dramatic spiritual awakening, and the next year he suffered a catastrophic spinal cord injury. He was diagnosed as a quadriplegic and told by doctors that he would remain so for the rest of his life. But today, Lex Luger is back on his feet, dedicated to mentoring others and sharing the incredible story of what God has done in his life.

JOHN D. HOLLIS is a veteran journalist who has covered both professional and college sports. He was the lead reporter for the *Atlanta Journal Constitution*'s story of WWE pro wrestler Chris Benoit's tragic end in 2007.